SWU–NAP– 026

UNIFORMS OF RUSSIAN ARMY DURING THE NAPOLEONIC WAR VOL.21

UNDER THE REIGN OF ALEXANDER I
EMPEROR OF RUSSIA BETWEEN 1801 AND 1825
THE IRREGULAR TROOPS

From the Viskovatov's greatest work:
"Historical description of the clothing and
arms of the Russian Army"

English translation by Mark Conrad

SOLDIERSHOP PUBLISHING

AUTHOR

Aleksandr Vasilevich Viskovatov born 22 April (4 May New Style) 1804, died 27 February (11 March) 1858 in St. Petersburg, Russian military historian. He graduated from the 1st Cadet Corps and served in the artillery, the hydrographic depot of the Naval Ministry, and then in the Department of Military Educational Institutions. He mainly studied historical artifacts and the histories of military units. Viskovatov's greatest work was the Historical Description of the Clothing and Arms of the Russian Army.

ACKNOWLEDGEMENTS

A Special Thanks to NYPL and other institutions for their kindly permission to use some images of his archives, collections or books used in our book.

Title: **UNIFORMS OF RUSSIAN ARMY DURING THE NAPOLEONIC WAR VOL. 21**
Irregular troops By A.V.Viskovatov. Serie edit by Luca S. Cristini. First edition by Soldiershop. August 2018 Cover & Art Design: Luca S. Cristini. Plates re-colorations by Anna Cristini.
ISBN code: 978-88-93273534

Published by Soldiershop publishing, via Orio 35/4 - 24050 Zanica (BG) ITALY. wwwsoldiershop.com

UNIFORMS OF
THE RUSSIAN ARMY
DURING THE
NAPOLEONIC WAR
VOL. 21

UNDER THE REIGN OF ALEXANDER I EMPEROR OF
RUSSIA BETWEEN 1801 AND 1825

*

THE IRREGULAR TROOPS

▲ *Russian irregular soldiers in Paris 1814*

HISTORICAL DESCRIPTION OF THE CLOTHING AND ARMS OF THE RUSSIAN ARMY - A.V. VISKOVATOV
(First English translation by Mark Conrad)

Soldiershop is glad to presents the complete collection of the great job made by A.V. Viskovatov dedicated to the uniforms and weapons belonging to the Russian army during the Napoleonic period, until 1825. The time we considered corresponds to the reigns of two Tzars: Paul I, who reigned since 1769 until his murder on the 23rd of March 1801, and his son Aleksandr Pavlovič Romanov, that with the title of Alexander I, sat on the throne until the 1st December 1825.

Our reprint in based on the original 19th century volumes, to be precise the volumes from 7 to 9 are dedicated to the reign of Paul I; this first part is distributed on 7 volumes, having a numbering from 1 to 7. From number 10 to 18 of the original volumes, the second part is dedicated to the Russian troops under Alexander I. These still being worked on and they will be soon ready, distributed on twenty volumes approximately. Our new edition, the first ever published in English, both on paper and digital format, boasts a large number of color plates, many of them unpublished and coloured by our team of expert artists and scholars of uniformology. Each volume is based on 50/70 plates, always accompanied by the original translated text which describes the uniforms, the organization and the armament of the Russian army of the period.

In this book we present the Russian irregular troops of the Napoleonic wars. A unique work in its genre, a must have in any respecting collection!

Aleksandr Vasilevich Viskovatov born 22 April (4 May New Style) 1804, died 27 February (11 March) 1858 in St. Petersburg, Russian military historian. He graduated from the 1st Cadet Corps and served in the artillery, the hydrographic depot of the Naval Ministry, and then in the Department of Military Educational Institutions. He mainly studied historical artifacts and the histories of military units. Viskovatov's greatest work was the Historical Description of the Clothing and Arms of the Russian Army (Vols. 1-30, St. Petersburg, 1841-62; 2nd ed. Vols. 1-34, St. Petersburg - Novosibirsk - Leningrad, 1899-1948). This work is based on a great quantity of archival documents and contains four thousand colored illustrations.

Viskovatov was the author of Chronicles of the Russian Army (Books 1-20, St. Petersburg, 1834-42) and Chronicles of the Russian Imperial Army (Parts 1-7, St. Petersburg, 1852). He collected valuable material on the history of the Russian navy which went into A Short Overview of Russian Naval Campaigns and General Voyages to the End of the XVII Century (St. Petersburg, 1864; 2nd edition Moscow, 1946). Together with A.I. Mikhailovskii-Danilevskii he helped prepare and create the Military Gallery in the Winter Palace.

He wrote the historical military inscriptions for the walls of the Hall of St. George in the Great Palace of the Kremlin. (From the article in the Soviet Military Encyclopedia.)

CONTENTS

*

RUSSIAN ARMY- IRREGULAR TROOPS
CHANGES IN THE UNIFORMS AND EQUIPMENT OF IRREGULAR FORCES FROM 1801 TO 1825.

I. Don Host. [*Donskoe voisko.*]

18 August 1801 – To replace the **uniform clothing** used in the Don Host since the time of EMPRESS CATHERINE II, the following uniforms were ordered to be introduced:
a) FOR DOMESTIC USE [*v domashnem bytu*]
Lower ranks—chekmen coat, or *kaftan*, of very dark-blue [*temnosinii*] cloth, with red cloth piping on the collar and cuffs; very dark-blue *sharavary* pants, with red trim along the side seams, allowed to be worn tucked into boots; short *boots* without spurs; a *cap* 5 vershoks [8-3/4 inches] high, of black fleece, with a red cloth top (Illus. No. 2425).
Officers—chekman coat, *sharavary* pants, and *cap* the same as for lower ranks, but the last item having a plume of white feathers that were black and orange at their base, and with the addition of cords and tassels (like shako cords) of silver, gold, and black silk (Illus. 2426).
b) FOR REGIMENTAL OR SERVICE USE [*v polkovoi ili stroevoi sluzhbe*]
Private Cossacks—chekmen coat of very dark-blue cloth, with piping in each regiment's own color as determined by the Host Ataman; very dark-blue *sharavary* pants with trim the same color as the *chekmen* piping; a *cap* the same as for domestic use, but with the addition of cords and tassels made from white thread, with a plume of white feathers that were black and orange at their base, and with a top the same color as the *chekmen* piping (Illus. 2427).
Non-commissioned officer [pyatidesyatnik or uryadnik]—the same as privates but the boots had spurs driven into the heels; white cords and tassels on the cap, mixed with orange and black, and white plumes with orange and black tops (Illus. 2428).
Officers—the same as for domestic use but boots with spurs driven into the heels and a cap with silver cords and tassels, without any admixture of gold and black silke (Illus. 2429).
In accordance with the long-standing custom of the Don Host, chekmens were ordered to bound at the waist with *girdles [kushaki]*, color unspecified, but insofar as possible uniform throughout each regiment. *Officers* were authorized ordinary sashes [sharfy] for specified occasions, tied the same way as girdles. In all regiments *sword belts*, pouches [sumki or lyadunki], and *crossbelts* were to be of black leather (with silver badges and chains for officers so desiring). No particular pattern

was specified for the *saber [sabel']*. *Sword knots* were to be as for regular light cavalry, and *lances [piki]* were left as before, with red shafts. *Saddlecloths [cheprakí]* remained in their current form, of very dark-blue cloth with trim or piping according to the color of the piping on the jacket. The Ataman's Regiment had sky-blue or light-blue [*goluboi* or *svetlosinii*] piping and trim, while girdles were white (Illus. 2430) [1].

The *chekmen* described here was to be worn in the cold months of 1 September to 1 May. For the rest of the time *jackets [polu-kaftany* or *kurtki]* of the same colors as the *chekmen* were authorized, worn tucked into *sharavary* pants (Illus. 2430 and 2431) [2].

11 January 1804 – On the **collars** and **cuffs** of their coats and jackets, generals and field and company-grade officers of the Don Host were allowed to have embroidered silver buttonhole loops, one on each side, adorned with leaves and flowers (Illus. 2432 and 2433) [3].

17 February 1809 – For ceremonial and parade occasions, Don Host generals were ordered to have on the collar, cuffs, cuff flaps, and pocket flaps of coats and jackets the same **embroidery** as established in 1808 for generals of regular forces, but in silver. Along with this, these ranks received a special kind of white **plume** or *chelenga*, as prescribed for general officers' hats in Hussar regiments under EMPEROR PAUL I and at the beginning of EMPEROR ALEXANDER I's reign (Illus. 2434). About this same time the following changes were made in Don Host uniforms: 1) silver **cords** were added to the shoulders of coats and jackets for generals and field and company-grade officers, twisted double like a plait, while lower ranks were given shoulder straps of very dark-blue cloth piped the same color as the piping on the collar; 2) feather **plumes** on the hats of officers as well as lower ranks were replaced by white hair plumes with—for officers and privates— black and orange at the base, and for non-commissioned officers—with black and orange at the top, and 3) the cords on **caps** were replaced by the same shako cords as used at that time by regular troops (Illus. 2434 and 2435) [4].

In 1812 – The **collars** of *chekmen* coats and jackets, instead of being diagonally open in front, began to be worn closed, fastened by small hooks and eyes, and in all regiments except the Ataman's piping and trim was established to be the same color: red. Also from this time non-commissioned officers were ordered to have silver galloon on the collar and cuffs (Illus. 2436) [5].

In 1814 – While Russian troops were in Paris, the plaited cords on the coats of Don Host generals and officers were replaced by silver **epaulettes** that followed the established rank distinctions for generals and field and company-grade officers (Illus. 2437 and 2438). In this same, while the **Ataman's Regiment** was in Paris, it lower ranks were ordered to have, on each side of the collar and on each cuff, two worsted sky-blue or light-blue buttonhole loops. Along with this, lower ranks in the regiment wore, instead of shoulder straps, worsted sky-blue or light-blue epaulettes with fringes, and the light-blue piping on collars and cuffs was removed (Illus. 2439) [6].

20 November 1815 – For increased uniformity and to be less of a burden on Don Host officers, its field and company-grade officers were ordered to have, instead of the current embroidery, silver **buttonhole loops** of the same pattern as in the Cavalier Guards Regiment, one on each side of the collar and two on each cuff (Illus. 2440) [7].

11 October 1816 – Field and company-grade officers of the Ataman's Regiment were ordered to have two silver **buttonhole loops** on each side of the collar instead of just one (Illus. 2441) [8].

20 November 1819 – The current white hair **plumes** on officers' and lower ranks' headdresses were replaced by the smaller elongated plumes used at that time in regular light cavalry regiments: silver for officers and of white wool for lower ranks (Illus. 2442) [9].

3 May 1822 – A HIGHEST Order directed lower ranks of the Ataman's Regiment to try to replace silk **crossbelts** and **sword belts** with leather ones of the same patterns as sword belts and crossbelts in the L.-Gds. Cossack Regiment [10].

II. DON COSSACK ARTILLERY. [*Donskaya kazach'ya artilleriya.*]

Before 1816 – Horse-Artillery companies in the Don Host had the same **uniforms** as the rest of the host, but on **11 February** of this year they were ordered to have:

Cossacks – *chokemen* coat, of dark-green cloth in the standard cossack style, with red cloth piping all around the collar and cuffs, and red shoulder straps on which were brass buttons for fastening these straps; dark-green *sharavary* pants without any trim; *girdle* of red cotton material [*bumazhnaya materiya*]; cossack *headdress* with a red bag, or top, and red cords, and with a white hair plume with a black base; iron *saber*, with a hilt of two arched guards, iron scabbard with two rings without bands or small hoops around them; *sword belt* of red Russian leather, with three iron rings (for slings), and three likewise iron buckles and an *ameter* [? unknown meaning – M.C.] of black Russian leather; *pouch [lyadunka]* (for the pistol) of black Russian leather, lacquered, with a brass badge on the cover; *pouch belt* of white leather; *pistol* with brass mountings, on a red wool cord (Illus. 2443).

Non-Commissioned Officer [Uryadnik] – all the same as for private Cossacks, but with gold galloon on the collar and cuffs, headdress cords with tassels in three colors: white, black, and orange; and with a black top to the plume (Illus. 2443) [11].

16 August 1817 – The following changes were made in the **uniforms** for *lower ranks* in the Don Cossack Artillery; *chekmen* coats were withdrawn, and in their place it was ordered to have *jackets* (for winter and summer), with black cloth collars and cuffs instead of dark green, and *shoulder straps* with the company number (1, 2, 3) in yellow cloth; one row of red cloth trim or stripe was added to the *sharavary* pants (Illus. 2444). *Officers* received uniforms in the same colors as prescribed for lower ranks; gold epaulettes with a silver company number and red backing, and silver cords on the headdress, without any admixture of black or orange silk. Officers of Companies No. 1 and No. 2 who had taken part in military operations in 1812, 1813, and 1814 were granted gold buttonhole loops to be worn on the collar and cuffs, while officers of Company No. 3, which remained on the Don, were not given this distinction (Illus. 2445) [12].

20 November 1819 – In the Don Cossack Artillery hair **plumes** on the headdress were replaced by smaller plumes of the same pattern as introduced at this time for Don Cossack regiments, but of red wool for lower ranks instead of white (Illus. 2446) [13].

III. BLACK SEA HOST. [*Chernomorskoe voisko.*]

Before 1816 – Clothing and weapons for Black Sea cossacks were not subject to any kind of mandatory rules, and the former kept almost the very same appearance as it had in the 18th century, and earlier as used by the Zaporozhian cossacks from whom Black Sea Cossacks were directly descended. Their **usual dress** consisted of a crimson, red, or—as they expressed it—"ruby" coat [*kontusha*] with the sleeves thrown back; *sharavary* pants, red boots, and a black (lamb's wool) cap with a red crown. With this dress each cossack shaved his head except for a long twisted lock [*zavernutaya chuprina*] behind the ear, and a long mustache. **Weaponry** consisted of: saber or *shashka*, dagger, pistols, musket, and lance. During the first half of EMPEROR ALEXANDER I's reign, uniforms of the pattern used in the Don Host began to be introduced into the Black Sea Host, with only the addition of two sleeves at the back, and without trim on the *sharavary* pants. On **11 February 1816** this **clothing** became mandatory. Along with this, Black Sea cossacks were prescribed the same weapons and the same accouterments as used in the Don Host. Besides the double sleeves and pants without stripes, Black Sea cossacks were distinguished from Don cossacks only in having white girdles instead of red, and instead of muskets the used lancer carbines carried on white deerskin crossbelts (Illus. 2447 and 2448) [14].

In 1820 – Following the example of the Don Host, the hair **plumes** on officers' and lower ranks' headdresses in the Black Sea Host were replaced by elongated pompons: of white wool for lower ranks, and silver for officers [15].

7 February 1822 – The carbines on white belts used by Black Sea cossacks were replaced by long-barreled **muskets** on plain black belts (Illus. 2449) [16].

IV. BLACK SEA COSSACK ARTILLERY. [*Chernomorskaya kazach'ya artilleriya.*]

At the same time as manadatory uniform clothing was introduced in the Black Sea Cossack Host, on **11 February 1816**, the Artillery of this Host, consisting of *Black Sea Horse-Artillery Company No. 6*, was prescribed **uniforms** and **weaponry** of the patterns used since 1817 by the 1st and 2nd Horse-Artillery Companies of the Don Host, but with two sleeves thrown behind on the back, without trim on the pants, and with the numeral 6 on shoulder straps and officers' epaulettes (Illus. 2450) [17].

In 1820 – The hair **plumes** on the headdresses of the Black Sea Cossack Artillery were replaced by small plumes of the same pattern and colors as those introduced at this time in the Don Cossack Artillery [18].

V. CAUCASIAN LINE COSSACK HOST. [*Kavkazskoe lineinoe kazach'e voisko.*]

This Host, from the very first when it was settled on the Caucasian Line through the end of EMPEROR ALEXANDER I's, borrowed its style of **clothing**, as well as **arms** and **horse furniture**, from the Mountain peoples with whom they were in contact [19].

VI. CAUCASIAN COSSACK ARTILLERY. [*Kavkazskoe kazach'ya artilleriya.*]

By a HIGHEST Order of **7 May 1817**, *Caucasian Line Cossack Horse-Artillery Companies Nos. 4 and 5* were prescribed the following **uniforms** and **weapons**:

Private cossacks - outer *caftan* coat or *chekmen* of Circassian style, of dark-gray cloth, trimmed along the edges with black wool tape half a finger in width that had a thin red cord running down it; collar and cuffs of black cloth, with red cloth piping; on the coat's breast black patches for 16 pistol cartridges; *inner caftan coat [ispodnii kaftan]*—of dark-green *burmet* [a coarse Persian cotton or baize – M.C.]; *sharavary pants*—of dark-green cloth in Circassian style, trimmed at the bottom in the same way as the *chekmen* with black tape and thin red cord; black *girdle* made from an unfinished leather strap with iron buckles and trimmed with thin silver and black silk galloon; black cloth *headdress [shapka]* of Circassian style, with a band of black lambskin and a red edge above the band, and thin red wool cord along the seams of the crown; *saber*—of Circassian style in a black leather scabbard with red edging, worn over the shoulder on a dark-blue sword belt of unfinished leather, with a brass buckle; *pouch [lyadunka]* (for 12 cartridges)—of black Russian leather, no lacquer or polish, worn on a black band [*tes'ma*], along with a *powder flask [natruska]*; *pistol*—of no definite pattern, in a black case or holster piped with thin red cord (Illus. 2451).

Non-commissioned officers [uryadniki] – the same as for private cossacks with the addition of silver and black silk galloon on the *chekmen's* collar and cuffs and above the headdress's fur trim (Illus. 2451).

Officers – all items the same as for non-commissioned officers but with the black tape on the *chekmen* and *sharavary* pants replaced by silver galloon with black silk, and with the addition to the seams of the saber scabbard and pistol case of the same thin galloon as on the girdle, over which when in formation they were ordered to wear the standard officers' sash (Illus. 2452) [20].

VII. ASTRAKHAN COSSACK HOST. [*Astrakhanskoe kazach'e voisko.*]

Prior to 1817 this Host had no defined uniform **clothing**, so that some of its cossacks were in *chekmen* coats, others in *arkhaluks*, and they were armed with sabers, *shashka* swords, daggers, muskets, pistols, lances, and bows and arrows, each according to his preferences and resources. Saddles and the rest of the horse furniture were Kalmuck or Kirghiz (Kazakh) patterns. On **11 October 1817**, a HIGHEST Order to the Astrakhan Host confirmed the following **uniforms** and **weapons**:

For *private cossacks* – jacket [*kurtka*], the same as for the Don Host but with lemon-yellow [*limonnyi*] piping instead of red, and without a number on the shoulder straps; *sharavary* pants—also of the Don pattern but with lemon-yellow trim; *girdle*—black; *headdress*—of the Don pattern with a top the same color as the piping; *saber, sword belt, cartridge pouch, pistol,* and *lance*—also of the Don patterns, but the sword belt being of black lacquered leather, and on the cover of the pouch the IMPERIAL monogram—A; a white cord for the pistol, mixed with black and orange (Illus. 2453); green shaft for the lance; a musket on a belt over the right shoulder.

For *non-commissioned officers [uryadniki]* – everything the same as for private cossacks but with silver galloon on the jacket's collar and cuffs; double stripes on the pants; sky-blue girdle; white tassels on the headdress cords, mixed with black and orange; black and orange top to the plume (Illus. 2453).

For *officers* – all as for officers in the Don Host, but with red cloth changed to lemon yellow, no number on the epaulettes, and silver galloon on the sword belt's and pouch's straps; sky-blue girdle (Illus. 2454) [21].

VIII. ASTRAKHAN COSSACK ARTILLERY. [*Astrakhanskoe kazach'ya artilleriya.*]

On **11 October 1817**, the same time as the above uniforms and arms were introduced into the Astrakhan Cossack Host, the exact same **uniforms** and **weaponry** were prescribed for the Host's assigned *Horse-Artillery Cossack Half-Company No 9*, with the addition of a yellow number 9—gold on officers' epaulettes—on lower ranks' shoulder straps, and without muskets for privates and non-commissioned officers [22].

IX. KALMUCK Host. [*Kalmytskoe voisko.*]

Formed at the close of **1811**, the *1st and 2nd Kalmuck Regiments* had *chekmen* coats, *sharavary* pants, and other pieces of **uniform**, as well as weaponry and horse furniture, all the same as that used in 1812 in the Don Host, with only the change of standard cossack headdresses to Kalmuck caps consisting of a yellow cloth crown somewhat like a lancer cap's, four vershoks [seven inches] tall, with a black sheepskin band, without any cords or plume. They also had the IMPERIAL Initial as a (white) monogram on the covers of their cartridge pouches and pouch belts, within a wreath and beneath a crown. Also, their saddlecloths had no trim (Illus. 2455). *Officers'* caps had bands of beaver fur, silver cords, and a white hair plume; saddlecloths with edges trimmed with silver galloon, and horse bridles with silver of silver-plated decoration (Illus. 2456) [25].

In 1814, following the example of the Don Host, field and company-grade officers of the 1st and 2nd Kalmuck Regiments replaced their silver shoulder cords with silver **epaulettes** (Illus. 2457) [24].

X. CHUGUEV COSSACK Host. [*Chuguevskoe kazach'e voisko.*]

Until 1803 the Chuguev Cossack Regiment kept all the same **uniform** items it had received under EMPEROR PAUL I when it was the 2nd Chuguev Cossack Regiment, and on **19 August 1803** there was a change only in colors, namely: black outer *kaftan* coat, or *chekmen*, and the black collar and cuffs of the (red) jacket were replaced by dark green, while the officers' yellow boots became black with thin silver cord trim around the upper edge (Illus. 2458). The regiment kept these uniforms, as well as the weaponry received under EMPEROR PAUL I, right up to its reorganization in 1808 from Cossacks to Lancers [25].

XI. BUG COSSACK Host. [*Bugskoe kazach'e voisko.*]

8 July 1803 – The newly established three Bug Cossack regiments were ordered to have the following **uniforms**, **arms**, and **horse furniture**:

Private cossacks – jacket of very dark-blue cloth, with white collar; white piping on cuffs and shoulder straps, and down the front opening and along the lower edge; likewise white buttons, in two rows, placed so that the distance between the two top ones was somewhat more than the two lower ones; dark-blue *sharavary* pants with a single strip of white trim; white *girdle*; *headdress* of black astrakhan, with a white cloth top, almost flat and not let down on one side as for Don, Black Sea, and Astrakhan cossacks; cap cords in two colors: white and dark blue, and a narrow white feather plume with black and orange feathers toward the bottom; *sword belt, cartridge pouch, and pouch belt*—black without any decoration; *saber, carbine,* and a pair of *pistols*—as for light cavalry; *lance*, with a very dark-blue shaft with the last four vershoks [7 inches] before the spearhead being white; very dark-blue *saddlecloth* with narrow white edging or trim; all *horse furniture* was black (Illus. 2459). Along with the uniform and armament described here, privates, being mounted, wore on a narrow black strap over the left shoulder a *whip* or *lash* [*plet' ili nagaika*], and had their pistols in black leather holsters fastened to the sides of the cartridge carrier [*patrontash*] worn in front on the saber belt. To each of the pistols was attached, with the help of a small brass ring on the butt, to the end of a black cord worn around the neck, as done with pistols in the cossack hosts mentioned above.

Non-commissioned officers – all the same as for private cossacks except for lances; plumes had black and orange feathers not at the bottom but at the top; tinned brass badge on the pouch lid; a similar IMPERIAL monogram on the crossbelt, and the addition of a a white silk sword knot on the saber which privates were not authorized (Illus. 2459).

Officers – uniforms exactly the same in color and style as for privates, but silver cap cords; pouch with a silver badge on the lid; pouch belt of lancer pattern with silver galloon that had dark-blue stripes down its sides, and with a silver HIGHEST monogram; silver sword knot, sash, and galloon on the saddlecloth; pistols in holsters under the saddlecloth (Illus. 2460) [26].

In 1812 – Lower ranks and officers were ordered to have: **collars** closed by small hooks; headdresses with the top falling down on the right side, as in the Don and other cossack hosts; **saddle pillows** [*podushki*], previously on top of the saddlecloth, were to be under the saddlecloth; non-commissioned officers were to have **lances**, the same as for private cossacks (Illus. 2461) [27].

In 1815 – In place of their previous very dark-blue shoulder straps with white piping, officers received silver **epaulettes** (Illus. 2462), and subsequently there were no changes in the uniforms, arms, and horse furniture of the Bug Cossack Host until it became part of the settled regular cavalry in 1817 [28].

XII. UKRAINIAN COSSACK REGIMENTS. [*Ukrainskie kazach'i polki.*]

5 June 1812 – Upon the establishment of the *1st, 2nd, 3rd, and 4th Ukrainian Cossack Regiments*, their personnel were prescribed the following **uniforms**, **weapons**, and **horse furniture**:

a) 1st Regiment:

Private cossacks – *jacket* of very dark-blue cloth, with raspberry collar, cuffs, and shoulder strap piping; gray *sharavary pants* with one raspberry stripe; lancer *girdles* of very dark-blue and raspberry stripes; cossack headdress of black fleece, with a raspberry top let down on the right side, and no other decoration of any kind; *saber* with an iron hilt, in a black leather scabbard with iron mountings; *sword belt, cartridge pouch,* and *pouch belt* of black leather, without decoration; *pistol* in a black leather holster, on a black strap; *lance,* as for lancers, with a black shaft and a pennant with a raspberry top half and a white lower half; instead of a saddlecloth, a black leather *pad* [*potnik*] and similar *pillow* [*podushka*]; gray cloth *valise* (Illus. 2463). In each squadron 16 men (flankers) had rifles [*shtutsery*], or if unavailable—muskets; each of these could be of any caliber.

Non-commissioned officers – the same as for private cossacks but excluding the lance and with the addition of silver galloon on the jacket's collar and cuffs (Illus. 2463).

Officers – uniforms of the same colors and cut as for lower ranks, but the jacket had one row of gilt buttons down the front, and gold epaulettes; very dark-blue *sharavary* pants instead of gray; headdress of black bearskin, with gold cords, gilt chin scales on straps, and a black leather visor; sword belt, saber, cartridge pouch, and pouch belt of lancer patterns, the first and last items with gold galloon; gold sword knot, silver sash; saddlecloth [*val'trap*] of hussar pattern, very dark-blue with raspberry piping and a gold HIGHEST monogram; pair of *pistols* in holsters, under the saddlecloth (Illus. 2464) [29].

b) 2nd Regiment – the same as in the 1st, except with raspberry changed to red (Illus. 2564).

c) 3rd Regiment – the same as in the 1st, except with raspberry changed to sky blue, and officers' appointments changed from gold to silver.

d) 4th Regiment – the same as in the 3rd, with sky blue changed to white (Illus. 2465) [30].

In 1815 – White cords and short white woolen plumes were added to the **headdresses** of lower ranks and non-commissioned officers. For lower ranks the plumes was black at the bottom or base, with a red pompon, while for non-commissioned officers they were black at the top with a non-commissioned pompon. **Jackets** had one row of buttons in front and two fringed epaulettes, both of the same color as the buttons on officers' uniforms. Along with this, privates as well as non-commissioned officers were ordered to have **sabers** in iron scabbards and a pair of **pistols** in holsters fastened to each side of the girdle. *Officers* were directed to have: headdresses with the same plumes as privates, with a pompon the same color as the cords, and with a metallic edge to the visor, the same color as the buttons; *sharavary* pants with two wide stripes [*lampasy*] with a row of piping between them, the same color as the collar; lancer saddlecloth, with trim and piping the same color as the collar (Illus. 2466). All these uniforms, arms, and horse furniture were used by the Ukrainian Cossack Regiments until their reorganizationin 1817 as Lancers [31].

XIII. URAL COSSACK HOST. [*Ural'skoe kazach'e voisko.*]

From 1801 through 1806 – *Lower ranks* of this host wore raspberry cloth *zipun* coat trimmed with white tape around the collar and at the bottom of the sleeves; sky-blue cloth *sharavary* pants with white trim on the side seams; leather *waist belt* carrying a leather *powder pouch* [*porokhovnitsa*], *bullet pouch* [*pulechnitsa*], powder *flask* [*natruska*] for the musket pan [*ruzheinaya polka*], and a small brass oil can [*smaznitsa*]; over the belt was a sky-blue cotton girdle; *cap* [*shapka*], of raspberry cloth, tall, with a black fur band; an iron *saber* on a black leather sword belt, and over the shoulder, on a black leather strap—a rifle [*vintovka*]. With these weapons the normal cossack *lance* was also used, with a black shaft decorated in three places with brass plates. The *saddlecloth* and *pillow* were of raspberry cloth trimmed with white tape, while the *bridle, breast strap,* and *crupper* were of black leather with white metal fittings (Illus. 2467). *Officers* had an *outer caftan* [*verkhnii kaftan*] of raspberry cloth with raspberry silk lining, trimmed around the collar, bottom of the sleeves, along the back

Typen Russischer Kosaken.
1813/14.

▲ *Russian Cossacks troops 1812-14*

seams, down the front opening, and along the lower edge with gold galloon 3/4 vershok [1-5/16 inch] wide; *inner kaftan [nizhnii kaftan]* or *beshmet* (also called an *arkhaluk*) of sky-blue cloth with five silver buttons [*pugovki*] on the left side, and with narrow silver galloon along the upper and side edges of the collar, down the front opening, and along the lower edge; *sharavary* pants of sky-blue cloth, with silver galloon along the side seams and lower edge; silk *girdle*, raspberry in color; cloth *cap*, also raspberry, with a band of black fleece; red Russian leather *sword belt*, with silver embroidery and fittings; *saber* with a curved blade, silver mountings on the scabbard, and a silver sword knot (Illus. 2467); the same *horse furniture* as for lower ranks, but with silver [32].

In 1806 – In accordance with its wish, the Ural Host was allowed to have **uniforms** of standard cossack pattern, dark blue in color, with raspberry for the piping on the jacket, stripes on the *sharavary* pants, and pompon on top of the headdress. Along with this change *lower ranks* began to wear dark-blue [*svetlosinii*] *girdles*; *sabers* of the pattern used at that time in the regular light cavalry, without sword knots, on a black sword belt; *carbines* on a black leather strap over the left shoulder; black leather *pouches [podsumki]* on a likewise black leather strap over the right shoulder (Illus. 2468); dark-blue *saddlecloths* and *pillows* with white trim; *bridles, breast straps,* and *cruppers* with brass fittings; *lances* as before. *Officers*, along with uniforms that were of the same color and pattern as established for lower ranks, wore silver twisted cords on both shoulders of the jacket; raspberry girdles, sword belts of red morocco with silver fittings; saber and sword knot like those prescribed for officers of regular light cavalry; pouch straps trimmed with galloon, silver with black edges, and with silver plates and small chains (Illus. 2468) [33].

In 1817 – **Officers** of the Ural Host were allowed to wear: silver epaulettes, silver buttonhole loops on the collar (one on each side) and the chekmen and jacket cuffs (two on each), and silver sashes. They were also allowed to have silver chin scales on their headdresses and a black leather visor with a silver edge (Illus. 2469) [34].

13

XIV. ORENBURG COSSACK HOST. [*Orenburgskoe kazach'e voisko.*]

8 June 1803 – The **Orenburg Permanent Cossack Regiment** [*Orenburgskii Nepremennyi Kazachii polk*], while otherwise having the same uniforms and weapons as Don Cossack regiments, was ordered to have: coat collars, cuffs, trim on the *sharavary* pants, and tops to the headdresses—all raspberry; white girdles; lances with a pennant [*khorunzhevka*, or *flyuger*] in two colors: raspberry above, and white below; dark-blue saddlecloths and pillows with raspberry trim (Illus. 2470) [35].

9 January 1808 – The Orenburg Cossack Host, along with the Orenburg Permanent Cossack Regiment, was allowed to have **uniforms** and **horse furniture** as prescribed for the Don Host. In this regard, it was left to the Host Ataman to distinguish regiments by choosing colors for piping on the collar and cuffs and for trim on the pants [36].

13 March 1808 – It was confirmed that the Orenburg Permanent Cossack Regiment would have the **raspberry** collar and trim established in 1803, and all officers of this host were permitted to have collars and cuffs with the same silver embroidery as prescribed for the Don Host (Illus. 2471) [37].

14 February 1816 – The Orenburg Cossack Host, with its uniforms identical to those of the Don Host, was ordered to have silver **buttonhole loops**, one on each side of the collar. This applied to all officers in the Permanent Regiment and for others—only those holding actual army ranks [38].

XV. ORENBURG COSSACK ARTILLERY. [*Orenburgskaya kazach'ya artilleriya.*]

28 February 1821 – Lower ranks of the Orenburg Cossack Artillery, consisting of *Horse-Artillery Cossack Companies Nos. 10 and 11*, were prescribed the same **uniforms** as Don Horse-Artillery Company No 3 had at this time, but with lancer pattern girdles, dark green with red stripes, and *sharavary* pants with two red stripes and piping. For officers, saddlecloths were dark green with red cloth trim and a gold IMPERIAL monogram under a crown (Illus. 2472) [39].

XVI. TEPTYAR REGIMENTS. [*Teptyarskie polki.*]

Until 1819 the *1st and 2nd Teptyar Regiments* modeled their **uniforms**, as well as accouterments and weaponry, on those of Orenburg cossacks, but on **4 July** of this year they were prescribed uniforms and arms as for Don cossacks, except shoulder straps were red; *girdles* were of two red stripes and one yellow; headdresses had a dark-blue top, and lance pennants had a white upper half and a lower half in a different color for each sotnia as determined by higher command (Illus. 2473) [40].

XVII. SIBERIAN LINE COSSACK HOST. [*Sibirskoe lineinoe kazach'e voisko.*]

In 1802 – By direction of Major General Lavrov, inspector of the Siberia Inspectorate, the Siberian Line Cossack Host, which up to that time had **no established uniform** or weaponry, was prescribed to be guided by the rules drawn up in 1801 for the Don Host regarding these subjects [41].

18 August 1808 – The **uniforms**, **weapons**, and **horse furniture** of Siberian Line cossacks was confirmed by HIGHEST Authority. In all ten regiments they were prescribed the same clothing as Don cossacks, with red piping on *chekmen* coats and jackets, a red top to the headdress, red trim on *sharavary* pants that had black leather sewn on the bottom of the legs. Buttons and shoulder straps were yellow, and girdles sky blue. Sword belts, crossbelts, and pouch belts, as well as the cartridge pouch itself, were of blackened leather; the saber was iron with a sword knot of red Russian leather; musket (for many still with a matchlock [*fitil'nyi zamok*], and pike with a black shaft. (*Note*: All Siberian cossacks (Line, Town, and Border in Eastern Siberia) wore pouches on the right side while the crossbelt, or bandoleer, was on the left so that the musket or carbine, carried from a hook on the belt attached to a ring and slide, hung butt downward on the left. In 1823 and 1824, when drawings of uniforms and arms for Siberian Town and Border cossacks, depicting a carbine on the left side and cartridge pouches on the right, were submitted for HIGHEST approval by EMPEROR ALEXANDER I, it was noted that if the example of regular light cavalry was followed, these items should have been reversed, with the pouch on the left and the carbine on the right. However, in this instance Siberian cossacks were permitted to carry them in the manner to which they had become accustomed.) Mongolian saddles were prescribed, of black, red, and yellow leather, with brass decorations on the front and rear arches, and all horse furniture straps were black, with likewise black strap tassels on the bridle, breast strap, and crupper (Illus. 2474). *Non-commissioned officers*, besides not having lances, were further distinguished by standard non-commissioned officer cap cords, pompons, and plumes. They had gold galloon on the collar and cuffs, gloves with cuffs, a cane, iron spurs driven into the boot, and a brass saber hilt and scabbard. In place of a musket they wore a pistol on the left side, in a black leather holster. *Officers* had the same distinctions from lower ranks as in the Don Host except for silver embroidery and sashes, which were not prescribed for the Siberian Cossack Host (Illus. 2475) [42].

8 April 1809 – Officers were allowed to wear **sashes** [43].

In 1812 – "To mark their zeal and good order when in HIGHEST service," the Siberian Line Cossack Host was granted **lance pennant colors** as follows: white top half and lower lengthwise stripe; lower half by regiment: *1st Regiment*—light green, *2nd*—sky blue, *3rd*—yellow, *4th* (Ataman's)—dark blue, *5th*—light raspberry, *6th*—brown, *7th*—gray [dikii], *8th*—red, *9th*—violet, and *10th*—green (Illus. 2476 and 2477) [44]. In this same year completely new patterns of **uniforms** and **weaponry** were confirmed for the Siberian Line Cossack Host, consisted of the following:

For private cossacks, to be worn when in unit formation – *jacket* in lancer style, of very dark-blue cloth, with red piping on the collar, red shoulder straps, cuffs, and skirt turnbacks, and brass buttons: one on each shoulder strap and four on each of the turnbacks; *chakchiry* pants of lancer pattern, of very dark-blue cloth with red stripes and piping, and with leather cuffs up to the knees; lancer *girdle*, of very dark-blue cloth with red trim along the edges; *shako [kiver]* of the same style as used by infantry up to 1812, but entirely of lacquered leather, with white cords, white pompon with a red center, brass scales on the chinstrap; *boots* with iron spurs; *saber* with iron hilt, similar scabbard, and sword knot of red Russian leather, with a white thread tassel; *sword belt* of black lacquered leather; *bandoleer* or *crossbelt* of the same leather, with brass buckle, slide, and end piece, and an iron hook; *pouch* (for 24 cartridges), also of black lacquered leather, with a round brass plate in the center of which was a two-headed Russian eagle, and with a iron ramrod for the pistol, on a black leather strap attached to the top part of the pouch; *pouch belt* of black lacquered leather attached by a small strap to the girdle, over the turnbacks; *carbine* of lancer pattern; *lance* of normal cossack pattern, with a black shaft and a pennant in regimental color; light cavalry *saddle*, with two holsters for pistols; *saddlecloth* and all *straps* of lancer pattern, the first of very dark-blue cloth with trim and monogram of red cloth; *greatcoat* of gray cloth, rolled and attached to the rear arch of the saddle (Illus. 2478).

For private cossacks in campaign uniform – all as for when in formation, but instead of dark-blue *chakchiry* pants with stripes and piping—gray riding trousers with only piping and no stripes, and with black leather trim at the feet; shako in an oilcloth cover, without cords or pompon, and instead of the leather lead [chumbur], a hair lead rope (Illus. 2478).

For senior non-commissioned officers [pyatidesyatniki ili starshie uryadniki] – the same as for private cossacks except for the carbine and lance, with the standard distinctions for non-commissioned officers in cap cords, pompon, and sword knot; gold galloon sewn onto all four sides of the collar and along the upper and side seams of the cuffs, and on the pouch belt—in brass, the IMPERIAL monogram within a laurel wreath (Illus. 2479).

For junior non-commissioned officers [mladshie uryadniki] - the same as for senior non-commissioned officers, but no galloon along the lower edge of the collar (Illus. 2479).

For officers – uniform items of the same patterns as those established for lower ranks, with gold epaulettes on red cloth backing; silver cords, pompon, stitching [proshvy] and tassel on the sword knot; *chakchiry* pants without cuffs; lancer *saber* on a black sword belt lined on its outer surface with gold galloon; *cartridge pouch* (for six cartridges) of black leather with a silver edge and HIGHEST monogram; *pouch belt* of the same black leather, with gold galloon and silver fittings as for lancers (Illus. 2479); *saddlecloth* as for lower ranks but with gold monograms.

Reserve cossacks (privates and senior and junior non-commissioned officers), along with the same weapons and horse furniture except for lance pennants and saddlecloths, which were not authorized for them, received *chekmen* coats of gray cloth, with a dark-blue collar and red shoulder straps; *sharavary* pants of gray cloth, with red piping and black leather reinforcement; *girdles* of gray with dark-blue; gray cloth *forage caps* cloth with a dark-blue cloth band, and with a black leather visor (Illus. 2480). The cap was prescribed to have sewn to it gray cloth ear flaps [naushniki] that if required could be folded up inside it, and a black leather rear flap [zatylnik] [45].

(*Note*: In a HIGHEST confirmed report from the Government Military Collegium dated 13 August 1808, regarding a new organization for the Siberian Line Cossack Host, *reserve cossacks* in this host were identified as those personnel beyond the authorized 500 men in each regiment (5000 for the entire host), intended as replacements for losses.)

XVIII. SIBERIAN LINE COSSACK ARTILLERY. [*Sibirskaya lineinaya ka-zach'ya artilleriya.*]

Until 1816 the Siberian Line Cossack Host's Artillery, consisting of two companies (from 4 August 1818 called Cossack Horse-Artillery Companies Nos. 7 and 8), adhered to the patterns used in this host's regiments in regard to **clothing**, **accouterments**, and **arms**, but on **25 August 1816** its personnel were ordered to have: dark-green jacket and pants (*sharavary*), the first having brass buttons down the front; black cloth collar, cuffs, and skirt turnbacks, with red cloth piping; shako as for cossacks but with red cords and pompon, with a brass plate of two crossed cannons and a grenade, as for Field Artillery, and with a black hair plume; chamois gloves with gauntlet cuffs; saber, sword belt, pistol, cartridge pouch, and pouch belt—all as for Cossack Artillery in the Don, Black Sear, and Orenburg Hosts, but all leather items being black; dark-gree saddlecloths with red trim (1-1/2 vershoks) [2-5/8 inches], monograms, and crowns (Illus. 2481). For officers, the monograms and crowns were gold. Up to 1818 the numbers on the **shoulder straps** were 1 for the first company and 2 for the second, but from that time they were replaced by the numbers 7 and 8 [46].

XIX. SIBERIAN TOWN COSSACK REGIMENTS and COMMANDS and COSSACK SETTLEMENTS. [*Sibirskie gorodovye kazch'i polki i komandy i kazach'i stanitsy.*]

Before 1822, when the small Cossack and Tatar commands in various Siberian locations (the Tobolsk, Siberian Tatar and Tomsk, Yeniseisk, Irkutsk, and Yakutsk commands) were reorganized as Town Cossack regiments, these commands had **no uniformity** in clothing or weapons, and each man was allowed to dress and arm himself according to his own means. Therefor some were armed with sabers and others with pistols. The same variety prevailed in regard to saddlery, which for the most part was of Kirghiz (Kazakh) style [47].

More regulated and uniform than the rest were the clothing and weapons of: the *Verkhneudinsk Cossack Command*, which joined the Trans-Baikal Town Cossack Regiment in 1822; the *Irkutsk Cossack Regiment*, in existence for the whole of EMPEROR ALEXANDER I's reign; and the *Yakutsk Cossack* Command, in 1822 detached to join the Yakutsk Town Cossack Regiment. The following information has been preserved reagarding these forces:

a) Verkhneudinsk Command.

From 1801 to 1815 – the cossacks and non-commissioned officers of this command had entirely dark-green cossack jackets; black *sharavary* pants with red trim (one row of stripes); yellow girdles; a yellow four-cornered hat like the Kalmuck caps described above, with a black cloth band (Illus. 2482), and a simple Mongolian saddle.

From 1815 to 1820 – very dark-blue jackets were used, with small skirttails and red collar, cuffs, and shoulder straps, similar to the jackets introduced in 1824 for Town cossacks in Eastern Siberia; gray pants with a single row of red stripes and sewn-on leather cuffs, without buttons; red girdles; boots with iron spurs; standard cossack headdresses with a red top and white (for non-commissioned officers with a mix of black and orange) cap cords, pompon, and hair plume; iron sabers with a lacquered black leather sword belt; the same leather was used for cross belts, cartridge pouches, and pouch belts; carbines; lances with black shafts and pennants that were white above and dark-blue below; saddles modeled after those for light cavalry, but with high arches with brass [*mednaya bronza*] along their edges; very dark-blue saddlecloths with red monograms and crowns (Illus. 2483).

From 1820 to 1824 – the uniform described above was replaced by very dark-blue *chekmen* coats with sky-blue collar, cuffs, and shoulder straps; gray *sharavary* pants trimmed with two rows of sky-blue stripes; headdresses with a sky-blue top (Illus. 2484). Sky-blue trim or edging was added to the dark-blue saddlecloths already in use [48].

b) Irkutsk Cossack Regiment.

In 1813 – The Irkutsk Civil Governor at that time, Treskin, directed that the Irkutsk Cossack Regiment have very dark-blue jackets, should straps of the same color, and red piping on the collar, cuffs, and down the front; very dark-blue pants to which were sewn black leather cuffs without buttons; dark-green cotton [*kitaichatie*] girdles tied as for lancers; cossack pattern headdresses of black cloth with a red top and white cords, pompon, and hair plume (Illus. 2485). Poorer cossacks were allowed to have just gray cloth greatcoats with two likewise gray collars, one standing and the other falling, and standard forage caps of very dark-blue cloth with a red band (Illus. 2485). The same greatcoats and caps were prescribed for other cossacks for wear when not on duty and in inclement or cold weather. Along with this uniform clothing, the regiment had to try to achieve uniformity in sabers, lances, pistols, accouterments (of black lacquered leather), and horse furniture, including dark-blue saddlecloths trimmed with white cloth monograms and crowns [49].

c) Yakutsk Cossack Command.

From 1818 – Lower ranks of this command began to take their uniforms partly from those of the Irkutsk Cossack Regiment and partly from the Siberian Line Cossack Host. As in the host, they had very dark-blue jackets with skirttails and red cloth collar, cuffs, and shoulder straps; very dark-blue lancer *chakchiry* pants with red double stripes [*lampasy*] and piping; lacquered black leather girdles; cossack headdresses of black cloth with are red top and white cords, pompon, and hair plume; boots with iron spurs; iron sabers; accouterments of lacquered black leather, including a cartridge pouch with a HIGHEST monogram of yellow brass. On the shoulder straps were fastened the tin Cyrillic letters YA. K. K. (*Yakutskaya Kazach'ya komanda*) (Illus. 2486). Officers had the silver should cords instead of shoulder straps; dark-blue silk girdles; black plissé headdresses with silver appointments; chamois gloves, cartridge pouches, and pouch belts, with silver fittings and galloon; the same sword knots as in the regular cavalry (Illus. 2486) [50].

22 July 1822 – The HIGHEST Confirmed Regulation for Siberian Town Cossacks established, among other rules, the following:

a) Cossacks were obliged to have their own clothing.

b) When in service, they were required to wear standard cossack dress, of special patterns determined by the provinces and regions [*po guberniyam i oblastyam*].

c) Yakutsk, Turukhansk, and Berzovsk cossacks were allowed to serve in clothing appropriate for their climate, and wear that to which they have long been accustomed, i.e. parkas [*parki*], etc.

d) In winter, all cossacks were allowed to wear warm clothing.

e) Cossacks were to have sabers and had to be armed with pistols and lances. These last had no pennants.

f) Junior non-commissioned officers [*mladshie uryadniki*] were to wear silver galloon only on the sleeves [i.e. cuffs – M.C.], while more senior non-commissioned officers [*pyatidesyatniki*, literally "leaders of fifty" – M.C.] had galloon on the collar and sleeves; officers were to have silver epaulettes and sword knots.

g) Headdress was to be the normal cossack pattern, with black all around and a dark-blue top.

h) Cossacks were required to have their own horses, with normal cossack saddles [51].

These regulations specifically applied to *Town Cossack Regiments*, of which there were the following:

1) *Tobolsk Regiment* – of Town Cossack commands in Tobolsk Province: Tobolsk, Tomsk, Turinsk, Berezov, Tara, and Surgut.

2) *Siberian Tatar Regiment* – of the Tobolsk, Tyumen, and Tomsk Town Tatar Cossack Commands.

3) *Tomsk Regiment* – of the Tomsk, Kuznetsk, and Narym. Town Cossack Commands.

4) *Yeniseisk Regiment* - of the Krasnoyarsk, Yeniseisk, and Turukhansk Town Cossack Commands.

5) *Irkutsk Regiment* – of the already existing regiment of that name.

6) *Trans-Baikal Regiment* – of the Nerchinsk and Verkhneudinsk Town Cossack Commands.

7) *Yakutsk Regiment* - of the Yakutsk, Okhotsk, and Izhiginsk Town Cossack Commands [52].

Apart from these regiments which received government support, there were established on their own resources small *cossack settlements [kazach'i stanitsy]* of Abakan and Pelym cossacks. Regarding these, the above-cited reorganization of Siberia in 1822 stated: "Settlement cossacks will not be required to maintain uniformity in clothing, but they are allowed to were standard cossack dress except without shoulder straps, with dark-blue collars. However, those men going out on patrols and guard duties must be armed with sabers, lances, and such firearms as may be conveniently borne." [52].

Regarding the uniform clothing and arms of the Town Cossack regiments ennumerated here, the following additional information has been preserved:

A) *Town Cossack regiments in Western Siberia: Tobolsk, Siberian, Tatar, and Tomsk.*

Subsequent to the above-mentioned Regulation for Siberian Town Cossacks, in 1824 and 1825 Town Cossack regiments in Western Siberia had dark-green jackets and *sharavary* pants, the first with raspberry piping and the second with raspberry stripes; black girdles, dark-blue tops to the headdress; black accouterments (Illus. 2487) [54].

B) *Town Cossack regiments in Eastern Siberia: Yeniseisk, Irkutsk, Trans-Baikal, and Yakutsk.*

In 1824, based on a HIGHEST confirmed proposal by the governor-general of Eastern Siberia, Lavinskii, the *Yeniseisk*

Cossack Regiment was prescribed very dark-blue jackets with small skirttails, light-green piping (for senior non-commissioned officers [*starshie uryadniki*] with the addition of silver galloon on the collar and cuffs, and for junior only on the collar); very dark-blue pants in *chakchiry* style, with leather cuffs sewn on up to the knees and light-green piping; shako of black astrakhan with a dark-blue top, in lancer style, with light-green piping (Illus. 2488); sword belts, sword knots, crossbelts, cartridge pouches (with a pistol ramrod), and pouch belt, all of black leather, the last with a monogram badge representing HIS MAJESTY'S name (in yellow brass), within an oval frame; lancer pattern sabers, carbines, and pistols; lances with black shafts, without pennants, saddles and other horse furniture of standard cossack patterns, except for saddlecloths, which were somewhat similar to those for light cavalry, of very dark-blue cloth with two rows of piping, monograms, and crowns, all in light green. In each sotnia 30 men were prescribed to have muskets instead of carbines. *Officers* and *reserve officers [za-urad-ofitsery]* were prescribed silver officers' sword knots. Along with the general distinctions for officer rank, they had silver epaulettes on light-green backing, with the Cyrillic letters Ye. K. P. (*Yeniseisk Kazachii polk*). Lower ranks had these letters on their shoulder straps, in light green [55].

In the same year of 1824, in accordance with a HIGHEST confirmed proposal by the Irkutsk civil governor, Zeidler, the *Irkutsk, Trans-Baikal,* and *Yakutsk Town Cossack Regiments* were given the same uniform clothing and weapons as the Yeniseisk Regiment, with different letters on officers' epaulettes and sewn on shoulder straps, which in the Irkutsk Regiment were ordered to be I. K. P., in the Trans-Baikal—Z. K. P., and in the Yakutsk—Ya. K. P. [56].

XX. STATION COMMANDS UNDER THE TROITSKO-SAVSK BORDER CHANCELLRY. [*Distantsionnyya komandy vedomstva Troitsko-Savskoi pogranichnoi kantselyarii.*]

These commands were the *Troisko-Savsk, Kudarinsk, Akshinsk, Chindan-Tarukuevsk, Tsurukhaituevsk, Gorbichensk, Kharatsaisk, Tunkinsk,* and *Nizhneudinsk Cossack Commands,* and before 1824 they did not have defined uniforms or weapons, although from 1816 to 1819 the Irkutsk civil governor of the time, Treskin, began to introduce uniformity in this regard. He directed that each cossack have: a very dark-blue *chekmen* coat, pants, and forage cap, with crimson cloth collar, coat piping, pants trim, and band around the cap; black accouterments, saber and carbine. In 1824, in accordance with a HIGHEST confirmed proposal by the Irkutsk civil governor, Zeidler, all these commands received the same uniforms and weapons as the Yeniseisk, Irkutsk, Trans-Baikal, and Yakutsk Town Cossack Regiments, but with blue [*svetlosinnii*] collar, shoulder straps, and girdle, with the Cyrillic letters P. K. V. (*Pogranichnoe Kazach'e Voisko* – Border Cossack Host) on the should straps (Illus. 2489) [57], and without a monogram on the cartridge pouch belt. During the whole of EMPEROR ALEXANDER I's reign the Tunguzsk and Bratsk, or, Buryat, commands had no prescribed uniform clothing or weaponry, but remained in their national dress, being armed with sabers, lances, and a *saadak* (quiver and bow case) with bow and arrows, of which every Tunguz carried 50, and every Buryat 40 [58].

In regard to uniforms and weapons of **other irregular forces** during EMPEROR ALEXANDER I's reign (1st and 2nd Nogai Regiments, Odessa Greek Infantry Battalion, Stavropol Kalmuck Regiment, Danube Cossack Host, the Simferopol, Perekop, Yevpatoria, and Theodosia Crimean Tatar Regiments, and the 1st and 2nd Bashkir Regiments), no satisfactory information has been preserved. (*Note:* A detailed listing of irregular forces from 1801 to 1825 is in Chapter XXIII of Volume 10 of this work.) The **Balaklava Greek Infantry Battalion** continuously kept the uniform given them during the preceding reign [59].

XXI. FLAGS OF IRREGULAR FORCES. [*Znamena irregulyarnykh voisk.*]

a) Don Host.

In 1803 this host was granted a flag with a light sky-blue center and dark sky-blue edges, surrounded in gold. In the middle, from each side, was a gold cross with a spear and shaft, and silver eight-pointed stars. On the edges was the inscription in gold: "*By the Grace of God We Alexander I Emperor and Autocrat of All the Russias, Moscow, Kiev, Vladimir, and Novgorod, Tsar of Kazan, Tsar of Astrakhan, Tsar of Siberia, Tsar of the Tauric Chersonese, Lord of Pskov and Grand Prince of Smolensk, Lithuania, Volhynia, and Podolia, Duke of Estland, Livland, Courland, and Semigalia, Samogitia, Karelia, and Tver, Yugor, Perm, Vyatka, Bolgaria, and others, Lord and Grand Prince of Novgorod of the Lower Land, Chernigov, Ryazan, Polotsk, Rostov, Yaroslav, Belozersk, Udorsk, Obdorsk, Kondia, Vitebsk, Mstislav, and all the northern lands Ruler and Sovereign of the Iveria, Kar-*

talia, Georgia, and Kabarda lands, of the Circassian and Mountain Princes and others the Hereditary Sovereign and Lord, Heir of Norway, Duke of Schleswig-Holstein, Stormarn, Ditmarsen, and Oldenburg, Sovereign of Ever, etc., etc., etc., grant this flag in place of that given in 1706 and renewed in 1746." On the reverse side: "To the Ataman and cossacks of Our Host, for their many and loyal services, especially that undertaken in 1705 during the Astrakhan troubles, in eternal and immortal memory, in the year of our Lord 1803, and of Our Reign the 4th year." The fringe, cords, and tassels of this flag were silver; the spearhead with EMPEROR ALEXANDER'S monogram in the center was gold; the pole was green, and the flag cloth was sewn to a crimson cloth wound around the pole (Illus. 2490).

In the same year of **1803** there was granted an all-white flag with the State coat of arms surrounded by the arms of Moscow, Kiev, Vladimir, Novgorod, Kazan, and Astrakhan, and by silver and gold wreaths and flowers. Around the flag, between panels outlined in gold, was the same inscription and above, but after the words "etc., etc., etc." was *granted this flag in place of that given in 1722 to the loyally subject Don Host for their service rendered during the war with the Swedes and for the permanent peace concluded with the Swedish crown. The year of our Lord 1803, and of Our Reign the third."* The fringe, spearhead, and all other adjuncts to this flag were exactly the same as for the above flag (Illus. 2491).

In the same year of **1803** there was a white flag similar to the preceding except for very insignificant differences in the images and the addition of four silver crosses on a blue field, surrounded in gold, In the inscription, after the words *"to the loyally subject Don Host,"* there followed: *"for their service shown in creating a permanent peace with His Majesty the Shah of Persia. In the year of our Lord 1803, and of Our reign the third."* Around the silver crosses on a blue field were the words in gold: *"Christ we glory in Your cross and sing Your Resurrection and glory that You are our God in the Holy Glorious Trinity."* (Illus. 2492). This flag was granted to replace that received by the Don Host from Empress Anna Ioannovna in 1733.

In the same year of **1803** there was a white flag with, in the center, a two-headed eagle on whose breast was a dark-blue shield edged in gold, with the gold monogram of EMPEROR ALEXANDER I. Above the wings alongside the crown in double gold circles were gold crosses, and between the outer and inner circles were words in gold, written in Church Slavonic characters: *"Christ we glory in Your cross and sing Your Resurrection and glory that You are our God in the Holy Glorious Trinity."* Around the flag, between gold stripes, was the gold inscription: *"This flag is granted in place of that given in 1764 to the loyally subject Don Host for their service rendered during the late Prussian war, 1803, of the reign of His Imperial Majesty, the All-Merciful Sovereign Emperor Alexander Pavlovich, All-Russian Autocrat, the 3rd year."* The fringe, spearhead, and other appurtenances to this flag were the same as for the above (Illus. 2493).

In the same year of 1803 the Don Host was given a white standard [*znachek*] with a two-headed Russian eagle, the gold script monogram of EMPEROR ALEXANDER, and various decorations. This guidon's fringe was silver, and all other appurtenances were the same as for the above flags (Illus. 2494).

In the same year of **1803** the Don Host was given two standards [*bunchuki*] of a pale straw color with raspberry edges. On it, between gold stripes, were gold and silver stars. On one standard was the archangel Michael in a rectangle, defeating the devil, and on the other, in the same kind of rectangle, was a silver cross surrounded by silver stars, and in the upper corner nearest to the pole, a hand coming out of the clouds. The fringe and other appurtenances were the same as for the above flags (Illus. 2495).

In the same year of 1803 the town of Novocherkassk [capital of the Don Host lands-M.C.] was granted a *coat of arms* [*gerb*] that was made up in gold and silver and with paints, on a rectangular dark-blue cloth surrounded by gold edging. It was fastened to a crossbar that hung by a cord below the spearhead of a normal flag pole. In the upper part of the cloth, above the coat of arms, was the gold inscription: *"Coat of arms of the Don Host town of Cherkassk, in Graciously granted by the Sovereign Emperor Alexander the First, on the 3rd day of October of the year 1803."* Below, under the coat of arms, was a description of the arms in gold letters: *"A shield, divided cross fashion into four parts, with a gold top in which is visible half of a black, two-headed, crowned eagle as it flies away; under this eagle on a red field in cross fashion: a gold mace [pernach] and two kinds of cossack scepter-like symbols of authority—a naseka and a bobylev khvost, and below, in a sky-blue field – another kind of mace [bulava], and two cossack symbols of authority—a bunchuk and another naseka; in the side parts, on a silver field, on the right side, are laid four flags crosswise: two white, one sky blue, and one red, with black eagles depicted on them, the flags being tied together in the middle with a laurel wreath, and on the left side above a river is a red fortress."* The cloth on the crossbar, the fringe, cords, tassels, and vertical pole were the same as for the above flags, while the spearhead was gilt with an IMPERIAL crown on top and the HIGHEST monogram in the center (Illus. 2496).

In 1807 *Khanzhenkov's* and *Sysoev's* Don Cossack regiments were each granted a white flag. On one side was a two-headed Russian eagle in an orange circle surrounded by gold wreaths, with a gold crown on top. On the other side in gold was the monogram of Emperor Alexander I in the middle of a gold sunburst. On each side of the flags was the gold inscription: *"For the feat at Schöngraben 4 November 1805, in a battle of a 5-thousand strong corps against 30 thousand of the enemy."* This flag had a gold fringe; silver tassels with an admixture of black and gold silk, hanging from St.-George ribbons; gild spearhead, with the cross of the order of St. George in the middle; green pole (of the pattern for standard poles in the Regular Cavalry, with gold longitudinal stripes (Illus. 2497).

In 1811 the Don Host was given a white flag with gold monograms, wreaths, and crowns in the corners, and with semicircles of St.-George ribbon on which in silver was the inscription: *"To the loyally subject Don Host for service rendered during the campaign against the French in 1807."* In the center of the flag, on one side, was a gold cross on a silver field surrounded by gold wreaths and flowers, and on the other—a two-headed Russian eagle on a gold field surrounded by gold wreaths and flowers. Gold fringe, silver cords and tassels; gold spearhead with an IMPERIAL monogram of the same in the center; pole as for the preceding flags (Illus. 2498).

In 1814 the *Ataman* Regiment was given a dark-blue flag with a painted image of the Savior surrounded by the gold inscription: *"God is with us, loosen your tongues and abase yourselves, for God is with us."* Around the flag is another gold inscription: "Awaken, Lord, Your mercy toward us, for we worship Thee, yea without fail for eternity" and "To the Don Host Ataman Regiment for bravery." This flag's fringe was gold; the spearhead and tassels were as for the 1807 flag described above; green pole with gold longitudinal stripes (Illus. 2499).

In the same year the same regiment received a white standard [*bunchuk*] with an image of St. George slaying a dragon and surrounded by the gold inscription: *"To the Don Host Ataman Regiment for distinguished courage."* This standard's fringe was gold, while the spearhead and tassels were as for the abov flags (Illus. 2500).

In 1816 *Dyachkin's* regiment was given a green flag with gold monograms in the corners, on a white field with gold crowns and wreaths. On one side of the flag, in an orange cirlce surrounded by gold wreaths, under a likewise gold crown, was a Russian two-headed eagle, and on the other side, in the same circle, was a crimson cross with gold edges and in a gold sunburst. On each side was the gold inscription: *"To Dyachkin's brave Don regiment."* The flag's fringe was gold; silver cords and tassels; gold spearhead, with a St.-George cross (Illus. 2501).

In 1817 the Don Host was given a flag similar to that granted in 1811 and described above, with the inscription: "To the loyally subject Don Host in recognition of deeds performed in the recent French war, in 1812, 1813, and 1814." The fringe and other appurtenances were the same as for the 1807 flag described previously (Illus. 2502).

In 1821 the regiments of *Zhirov, Vlasov 3, Ilovaiskii 11, and Grekov 18* each received a white flag with straw-colored corners, with gold eagles, monograms, wreaths, crowns, and stripes, and the gold inscription: *"For distinguished courage in defeating the enemy."* The fringes on these flags were gold while the tassels, spearheads, and poles were as for the 1807 flags (Illus. 2503).

In the same year of **1821** the regiments of *Melnikov 4* and *Melnikov 5* each received a flag similar to the preceding but with the inscription: *"In recognition of outstanding deeds performed in the battles at Craone and Laon during the recent war against the French."* The fringes on these flags were gold, the cords and tassels silver; gold spearhead with a two-headed eagle in the center; green pole with gold longitudinal stripes (Illus. 2504).

b) Black Sea Host.

In 1803 this host was granted 12 regimental flags in the form of standards [*znachki*] in the following colors: 6 with orange above, dark-blue below, and 6 just the opposite—dark-blue above and orange below. In the center of each flag was a red cross within gold rays. The fringe around the flag was gold; cords and tassels were silver; a gilt spearhead had the monogram initials of EMPEROR ALEXANDER; white poles (Illus. 2505).

c) Astrakhan Cossack Host.

In 1818 this host was granted a white flag with straw-colored corners and a gold image of a two-headed Russian eagle in the center. Monograms in the corners, wreaths, crowns, and edging around the field were all gold. Silver cords and tassels; gold spearhead; white pole (Illus. 2506).

d) Kalmuck Regiments.

During military operations in 1812, 1813, and 1814, the *2nd Kalmuck Regiment* had an old straw-colored flag with painted inscriptions and gold images of an armed horseman, beasts, and birds. This flag was fastened to a red pole in three places, and had a red border and three hanging ribbons, likewise red. The pole's gilded spearhead was decorated with a kind of long tassel composed of four elongated rectangles colored green, pink, crimson, yellow, and sky blue. Below the spearhead along the pole was affixed another decoration in sky blue, white, crimson, yellow, and green (Illus. 2507). The figures on the flag had the following significance: *man on a white horse* – the Kalmuck deity called *Daiachi Tengry*, the patron of war and warriors, giving aide in battle and enabling victories; *beasts and birds* – this deity's attributes, the first having the meanings of power, strength, speed, and overlordship of the earth, and the second—the same qualities plus sway over the heavens; *flag in the horseman's hand* – the banner of victory; *whip in the horseman's hand* – shows the path ahead for the horse; *red branches at the horse's head and hooves* – it's fiery gallop; *beasts behind the horseman's shoulders* – the terrifying invasion by the deity and, at the same time, his accompanying bodyguards. This flag's pole was 2-1/2 (17-1/2 feet) sazhens long. (*Note:* At the 2nd Kalmuck Regiment's departure on campaign in 1812, as well as upon its return to its home *ulus* in 1814, special religious rites were performed. Sacrifices were offered in the form of smoking various fragrant grasses and lighting many candles. After this ceremony in 1814, the flag was placed in the main *khurul* or *syum*, i.e. the Kalmucks' national temple, where it remains to this day.)

e) Bashkir Host.

In 1805 the *9th Bashkir Canton* was granted a dark-blue flag in the center of which was a gold HIGHEST monogram surrounded by a likewise gold, star-shaped burst of rays. In the corners were silver stars. This flag had gold fringe, silver cords and tassels, a gold spearhead with a HIGHEST monogram, and a white pole (Illus. 2508).

f) Bug Cossack Host.

In 1804 the *1st, 2nd, and 3rd Bug Cossack Regiments* were granted flags exactly like those received in 1803 by the Black Sea Cossack Regiment, but colored as 1 white and 4 black for each of these regiments (Illus. 2509).

g) Nogai Regiments.

In 1802 flags were prepared for the *1st and 2nd Nogai Regiments*, similar to the preceding but completely plain, without cross or star burst. Each regiment had 1 white and 4 black flags (Illus. 2510).

h) Siberian Line Cossack Host.

In 1809 this host was granted (one for each regiment) 10 flags of the pattern received in 1803 and 1804 by Black Sea and Bug cossack regiments, but with a green upper part and raspberry below (Illus. 2511) [60].

▲ *Battle of monastere of Kolotz 19 October 1812*

NOTES

(1) *Complete Collection of Laws* [*Polnoe Sobranie Zakonov*, henceforth PSZ], Vol. XLIV, pg. 58, No. 19,983, and contemporary drawings.

(2) Ibid.

(3) Ibid., No. 20,901, and information and drawings received from the Don Host Government Ataman, 26 November 1846, No. 498.

(4) Ibid., No. 23,492, contemporary drawings, and information from contemporaries.

(5) Contemporary drawings and information from contemporaries.

(6) Instruction of Host Ataman Graf Platov to Government Ataman Ilovaiskii 5, 30 April 1816.

(7) PSZ, Vol. XLIV, pg. 102, No. 26,002.

(8) Instruction for Host Ataman Graf Platov to the commander of the Ataman Regiment, Major General Grekov 18, 11 October 1816, and contemporary drawings.

(9) PSZ, Vol. XLIV, pg. 137, No. 17,990.

(10) Announcement by the Chief of HIS IMPERIAL MAJESTY'S Main Staff to the Chairman of the Committee for Don Host organization, General-Adjutant Chernyshev, 3 May 1822.

(11) PSZ, Vol. XLIV, pg. 136, No. 26,138.

(12) Ibid., and information received from the DON HOST GOVERNMENT ATAMAN, 26 November 1846, No. 498.

(13) PSZ, Vol. XLIV, pg. 137, No. 17,990, and contemporary drawings.

(14) Information received from the Black Sea Cossack Host, and HIGHEST Confirmed description of its uniforms and accouterments, 11 February 1816.

(15) Information from the War Ministry's Commissariat Department.

(16) Memorandum to the Black Sea Host Chancellery from the Field Ataman of Don Cossack Regiments in the Separate Caucasus Corps, Major General Vlasov, 2 March 1822, No. 642.

(17) PSZ, Vol. XLIV, pg. 136, No. 26,138.

(18) Information received from the War Ministry's Commissariat Department.

(19) Memorandum of the command-in-chief of the Separate Caucasus Corps to the Chief of Ways of Communications and Public Buildings, 4 August 1846, No. 1859.

(20) PSZ, Vol. XLIV, pgs. 118 and 119, No. 26,839.

(21) Submission of the Astrakhan Cossack Host's administration office to the Host officer commanding officer, Colonel Popov, 8 October 1846, No. 3004, and a directive from HIS IMPERIAL MAJESTY'S Main Staff's Inspection Department to the Lieutenant Dontsov of the Astrakhan Cossack Host, 29 January 1818, No. 682.

(22) Ditto.

(23) Information and drawings provided by the Kalmuck ruler of the Khomoutov *ulus*, Colonel Prince Serbedzhas-Tyumenev, who commanded the 2nd Kalmuck Regiment during the 1812, 1813, and 1814 campaigns, and in the years following.

(24) The same information and drawings.

(25) PSZ, Vol. XLIV, pg. 58, № 20,901.

(26) PSZ, Vol. XXVII, pg. 650, No. 20,789, and information and drawings received in 1847 from the Inspector of Reserve Cavalry and from the Kherson Civil Governor.

(27) The same information and drawings.

(28) The same information.

(29) PSZ, Vol. XXXII, pg. 339, No. 25,129, and information and drawings received in 1847 from the Inspector of Reserve Cavalry.

(30) The same information and drawings.

(31) The same information and drawings.

(32) Information and drawings provided by the commander of the 23rd Infantry Division in the absence of the commander of the Separate Orenburg Corps, 11 March 1848, No. 434.

(33) The same information and drawings, and a directive of the Orenburg Military Governor to the Host Chancellery of

the Ural Host, 18 November 1806, No. 498.

(34) The same information and drawings, and a directive of the Orenburg Military Governor to the Host Ataman of the Ural Host, 19 July 1817, No. 795.

(35) HIGHEST Confirmed report of the State Military Collegium on the organization of the Orenburg Cossack Host and the Orenburg Permanent Cossack Regiment, 8 June 1803, point 12.

(36) PSZ, Vol. XLIV, pg. 59, No. 22,760.

(37) Directive of the Host Ataman of the Don Host to the Host Ataman of the Orenburg Host, Colonel Ugletskii, 13 March 1808, No. 393.

(38) Directive of the Orenburg Military Governor and Commander of the Separate Orenburg Corps to the Host Ataman of the Orenburg Host, 14 February 1816, No. 319.

(39) HIGHEST confirmed table of uniforms, weapons, and accouterments for one Orenburg Horse-Artillery company, 28 February 1821, and drawings received in 1848 from the commander of the Separate Orenburg Corps.

(40) Information received from the War Ministry's Commissariat Department.

(41) Information and drawings provided by the commander of the Separate Siberian Corps, 5 January 1847, No. 34.

(42) The same information and drawings.

(43) PSZ, Vol. XXX, pg. 947, No. 23,619.

(44) Instruction of Lieutenant General Glazenap to the Host Chancellery of the Siberian Line Cossack Host, 7 July 1812, No. 575.

(45) The information and drawings referred to in Notes 41 and 42.

(46) *Collection of Laws and Regulations Relating to the Military Administration*, 1816, Book III, pg. 153 et seq., and information received from the War Ministry's Commissariat Department.

(47) Information from the commander of the Separate Siberian Corps, 23 August 1849, No. 5079.

(48) Information delivered in 1847 from the officer in charge of the Trans-Baikal Town Cossack Regiment.

(49) Instructions of Irkutsk Civil Governor Treskin to the officer in charge of the Irkutsk Cossack Regiment, 6 June 1813.

(50) Report of the official in charge of Irkutsk Province to the acting Governor-General of Eastern Siberia, 29 July 1848, No. 4318.

(51) PSZ, Vol. XXVIII, No. 29,131, pg. 539, §§ 102-109.

(52) *Historical Description of the Clothing and Arms of the Russian Army*, Vol. X, Chapter XXII, and PSZ, Vol. XXXVIII, No. 29,131, pg. 532, §§ 6-15.

(53) Ibid., pg. 544, § 182.

(54) Information and drawings provided by the commander of the Separate Siberian Corps, 23 August 1849, No. 5079.

(55) Directive of the Irkutsk Civil Governor to the acting Ataman of the Yeniseisk Cossack Regiment, 28 February 1824, No. 225, and drawings enclosed with this directive.

(56) Note on the uniform clothing of Town and Border cossacks in Irkutsk Province, sent by Irkutsk Civil Governor Zeidler to the Governor-General of Eastern Siberia in a report of 15 March 1823, No. 736, and a submission to him by the Governor-General, 15 February 1824, No. 108.

(57) The same information as in the preceding Note, a report by the official in charge of Irkutsk Province, Karpinskii, to the Governor-General of Eastern Siberia, 17 April 1847, and drawings accompanying a directive of Collegial Assessor Zeidler to Tsurukhaituevsk Border Warden 12th class Razgildeev.

(58) The report of 17 April 1847 referenced in the preceding Note.

(59) Information received from the Balaclava Infantry Battalion.

(60) All information included in this section, as well as the accompanying drawings of flags, are taken from information and drawings provided by the Irregular Forces and the War Ministry's Commissariat Department.

РИСУНКИ
ОДЕЖДЫ и ВООРУЖЕНІЯ
РОССІЙСКИХЪ
ВОЙСКЪ
1801-1825.

PLATES LIST OF ILLUSTRATIONS

2470. Officer and Cossack. Orenburg Permanent Cossack Regiment, 1803-1808.

2471. Officer. Orenburg Permanent Cossack Regiment, 1808-1809.

2472. Company-Grade Officer and Non-Commissioned Officer [*Uryadnik*]. Orenburg Cossack Artillery, 1821-1825.

2473. Private. Teptyar Regiments, 1819-1825.

2474. Cossack. Siberian Line Cossack Host, 1808-1812.

2475. Officer and Non-Commissioned Officer [*Uryadnik*]. Siberian Line Cossack Host, 1808-1812.

2476. Lance pennants for cossack regiments of the Siberian Line Cossack Host, granted in 1812. 1st Regiment. 2nd Regiment. 3rd Regiment. 4th Regiment. 5th Regiment.

2477. 6th Regiment. 7th Regiment. 8th Regiment. 9th Regiment. 10th Regiment.

2478. Cossacks. Siberian Line Cossack Host, 1812-1825.

2749. Company-Grade Officer, Senior and Junior Non-Commissioned Officers [*Starshii i Mladshii Uryadniki*]. Siberian Line Cossack Host, 1812-1825.

2480. Reserve Cossack. Siberian Line Cossack Host, 1812-1825.

2481. Cossack and Company-Grade Officer. Siberian Line Cossack Artillery, 1816-1825

2482. Cossack. Verkhneudinsk Cossack Command, 1801-1815.

2483. Cossack. Verkhneudinsk Cossack Command, 1815-1820.

2484. Cossack. Verkhneudinsk. Cossack Command, 1820-1824.

2485. Cossacks. Irkutsk Cossack Regiment, 1813-1825.

2486. Officer and Cossack. Irkutsk Cossack Command, 1818-1824.

2487. Cossack. Town Cossack Regiments of Western Siberia: Tobolsk, Siberian Tatar, and Tomsk, 1824-1825.

2488. Senior Non-Commissioned Officer and Cossack. Town Cossack Regiments of Eastern Siberia: Yeniseisk, Irkutsk, Trans-Baikal, and Yakutsk, 1824-1825.

2489. Cossack. Station Commands under the Troitsko-Savsk Border Chancellry, 1824-1825.

2490. Flag granted to the Don Host in 1803.

2491. Don Host Flag, granted in 1803.

2492. Don Host Flag, granted in 1803.

2493. Flag of the Don Host, granted in 1803.

2494. Don Host Flag [*Znachek*], granted in 1803.

2495. Don Host Standards [*Bunchuki*], granted in 1803.

2496. Novocherkask city coat-of-arms, granted in 1803.

2497. Flag of Khanzhenkov's Don Cossack Regiment, granted in 1807. *Note: An identical flag was granted at the same time to Sysoev's Don Regiment.*

2498. Don Host Flag, granted in 1811.

2499. Flag of the Don Host Ataman's Regiment, granted in 1814.

2500. Standard [*Bunchuk*] of the Don Host Ataman Regiment, granted in 1814.

2501. Flag of Dyachkin's Don Cossack Regiment, granted in 1816.

2502. Don Host Flag, granted in 1817.

2503. Flag of Zhirov's Don Cossack Regiment, granted in 1821. *Note: The same Flags were granted at the same time to the regiments of Vlasov 3rd, Ilovaiskii 11th, and Grekov 18th.*

2504. Flag of Mel'nikov 4th's Don Cossack Regiment, granted in 1821. *Note: The same exact Flag was at the same time granted to Mel'nikov 5th's Regiment.*

2505. Flags of the Black Sea Cossack Host, granted in 1803.

2506. Flag of the Astrakhan Cossack Host, granted din 1818.

2507. Flag formerly with the 2nd Kalmuck Regiment during the campaigns of 1812, 1813, and 1814.

2508. Flag of the 9th Bashkir Canton, granted in 1805.

2509. Flags of the Bug Cossack Regiments, granted in 1804.

2510. Flags of the Nogai Regiments, granted in 1802.

2511. Flag of the Siberian Line Cossack Host, granted in 1809.

Cossacks. Don Host, 1801-1809.

Officer. Don Host, 1801-1804.

Cossack. Don Host, 1801-1809.

2428

Non-Commissioned Officer [Uryadnik]. Don Host, 1801-1809.

31

Officer. Don Host, 1801-1804.

Cossack and Non-Commissioned Officer. Don Ataman Cossack Regiment, 1801-1809.

Officers. Don Host, 1801-1804.

Officers. Don Host, 1801-1809.

Officers' coat embroidery for the Don Host, established 14 January 1804.

General. Don Host, 1809-1812.

Officer and Non-Commissioned Officer. Don Host, 1809-1812.

Officer and Non-Commissioned Officer. Don Host, 1812-1814.

Field and Company-Grade Officers. Don Host, 1814-1815.

General. Don Host, 1814-1825.

Cossack. Don Ataman Cossack Regiment, 1814-1819.

Field-Grade Officer. Don Host, 1815-1819.

Company-Grade Officer. Don Ataman Cossack Regiment, 1816-1819.

Cossack, Don Ataman Cossack Regiment, and Field-Grade Officer, Don Host. 1819-1825.

Non-Commissioned Officer and Cossack. Don Cossack Artillery, 1816-1817.

Cossack. Don Cossack Artillery, 1817-1819.

2445

Company-Grade Officers. Don Cossack Artillery, 1817-1819.

Non-Commissioned Officer. Don Cossack Artillery, 1819-1825.

Cossack and Non-Commissioned Officer [Uryadnik]. Black Sea Host, 1816-1820.

Field-Grade Officer. Black Sea Host, 1816-1820.

Cossack. Black Sea Host, 1822-1825.

Non-Commissioned Officer [Uryadnik] and Company-Grade Officer. Black Sea Host, 1816-1820.

Non-Commissioned Officer [Uryadnik] and Cossack. Caucasian Cossack Artillery, 1817-1825.

Officer. Caucasian Cossack Artillery, 1817-1825.

Cossack and Non-Commissioned Officer [Uryadnik]. Astrakhan Cossack Host, 1817-1825.

Company-Grade Officer. Astrakhan Cossack Host, 1817-1825.

Private, Kalmuck Regiments, 1812-1825.

Officer. Kalmuck Regiments, 1812-1814.

Field-Grade Officer. Kalmuck Regiments, 1812-1825.

Officer and Cossack. Chuguev Cossack Regiment, 1803-1808.

Cossack and Non-Commissioned Officer [Uryadnik]. Bug Cossack Host, 1803-1812.

Officer. Bug Cossack Host, 1803-1812.

Non-Commissioned Officer [Uryadnik]. Bug Cossack Host, 1812-1817.

Company-Grade Officer. Bug Cossack Regiment, 1815-1817.

Cossack. 1st Ukrainian Cossack Regiment, 1812-1815.

Non-Commissioned Officer [Uryadnik] of the 1st and Company-Grade Officer of the 2nd Ukrainian Cossack Regiments, 1812-1815.

Cossack of the 3rd and Company-Grade Officer of the 4th Ukrainian Cossack Regiments, 1812-1815.

2466

Company-Grade Officer of the 1st and Non-Commissioned Officer [Uryadnik] of the 14th Ukrainian Cossack Regiments, 1815-1817.

Officer and Cossack. Ural Cossack Host, 1801-1806.

Officer and Cossack. Ural Cossack Host, 1806-1812.

Company-Grade Officer. Ural Cossack Host, 1817-1825.

2470

Officer and Cossack. Orenburg Permanent Cossack Regiment, 1803-1808.

Officer. Orenburg Permanent Cossack Regiment, 1808-1809.

Company-Grade Officer and Non-Commissioned Officer [Uryadnik]. Orenburg Cossack Artillery, 1821-1825.

Private. Teptyar Regiments, 1819-1825.

Cossack. Siberian Line Cossack Host, 1808-1812.

Officer and Non-Commissioned Officer [Uryadnik]. Siberian Line Cossack Host, 1808-1812.

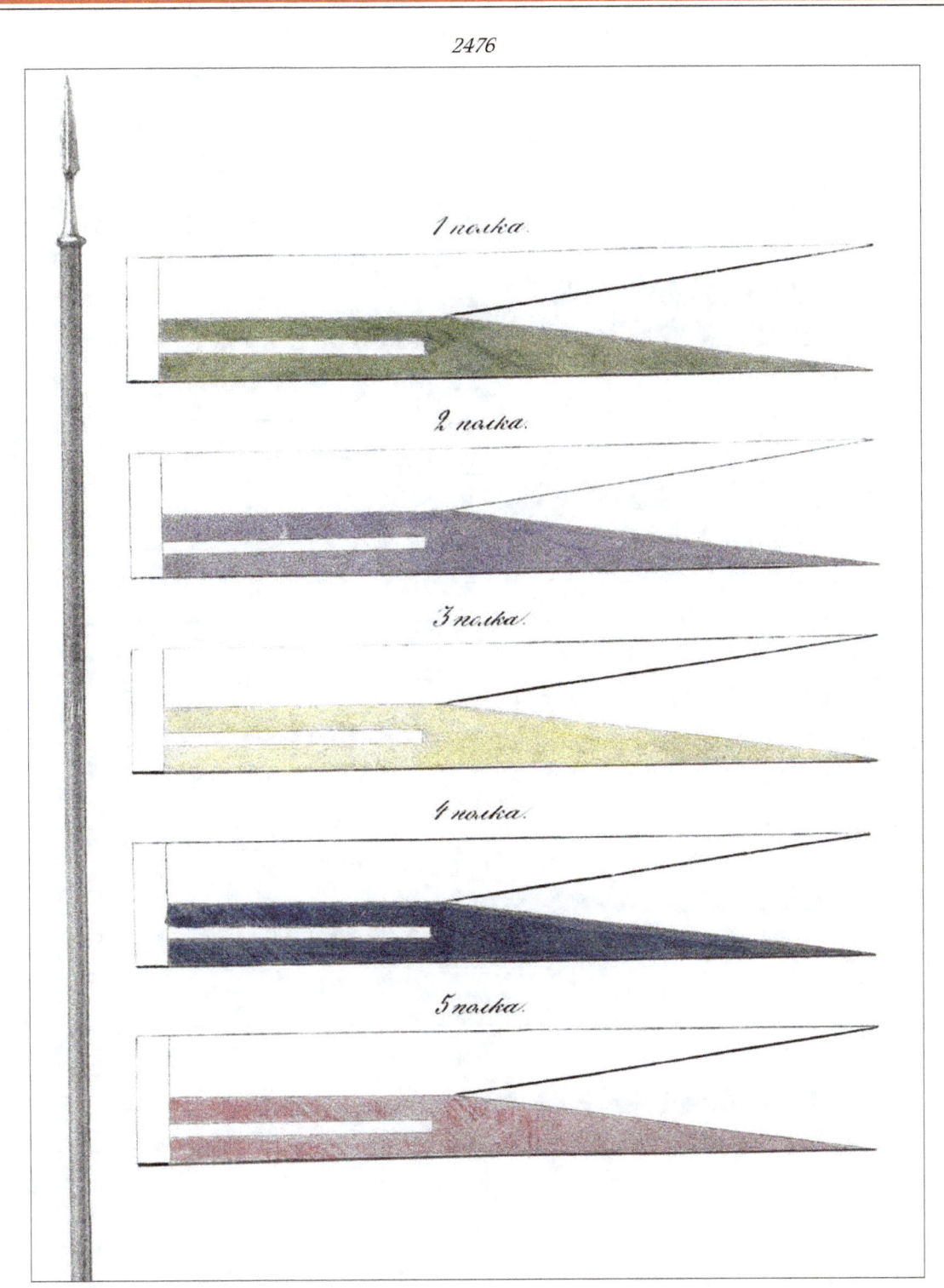

1 полка.

2 полка.

3 полка.

4 полка.

5 полка.

Lance pennants for cossack regiments of the Siberian Line Cossack Host, granted in 1812. 1st Regiment. 2nd Regiment. 3rd Regiment. 4th Regiment. 5th Regiment.

2477

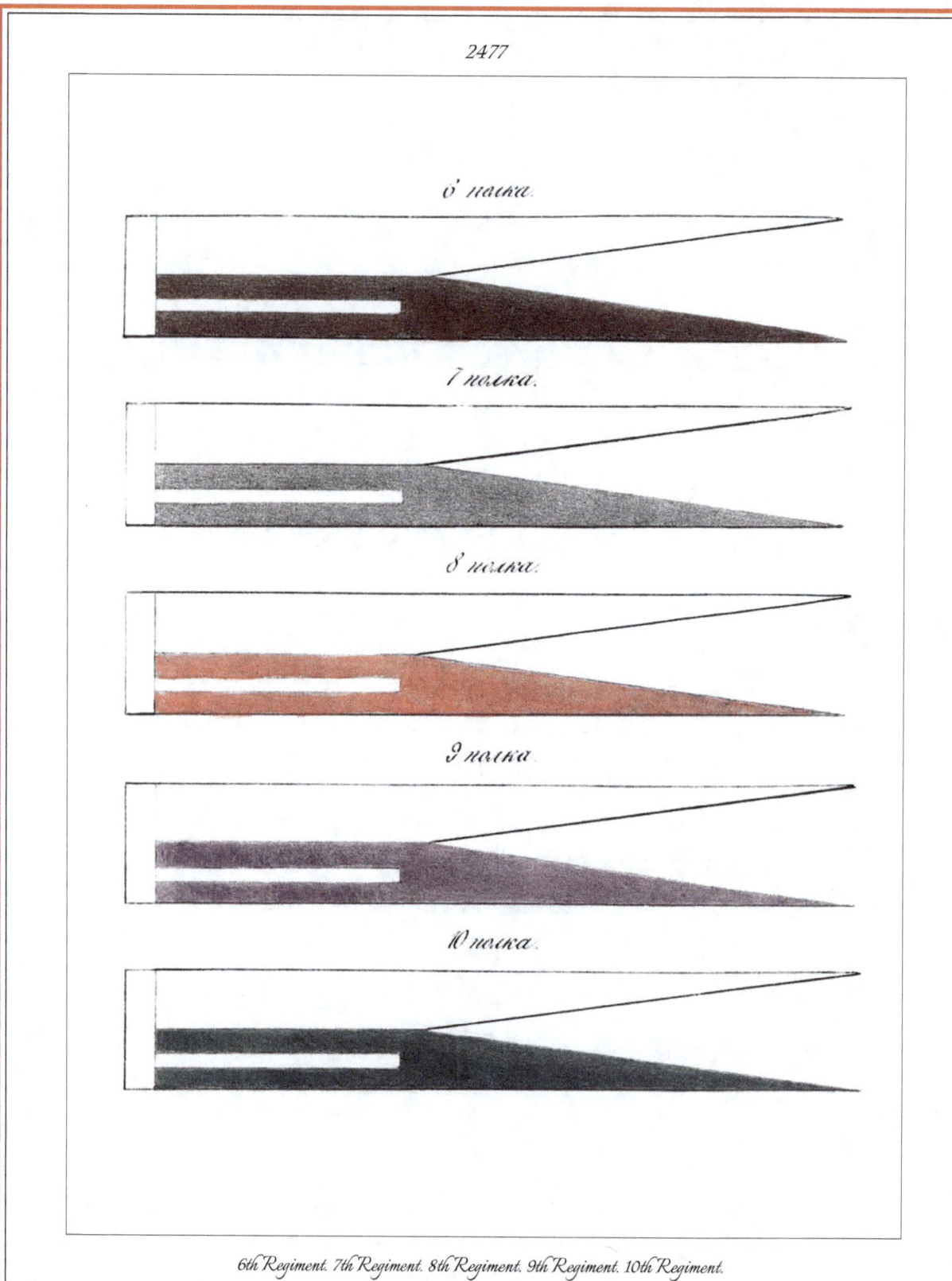

6th Regiment. 7th Regiment. 8th Regiment. 9th Regiment. 10th Regiment.

Cossacks. Siberian Line Cossack Host, 1812-1825.

Company-Grade Officer, Senior and Junior Non-Commissioned Officers Siberian Line Cossack Host, 1812-1825.

Reserve Cossack. Siberian Line Cossack Host, 1812-1825.

Cossack and Company-Grade Officer. Siberian Line Cossack Artillery, 1816-1825

Cossack. Verkhneudinsk Cossack Command, 1801-1815.

Cossack. Verkhneudinsk Cossack Command, 1815-1820.

Cossack. Verkhneudinsk. Cossack Command, 1820-1824.

Cossacks. Irkutsk Cossack Regiment, 1813-1825.

Officer and Cossack. Irkutsk Cossack Command, 1818-1824.

Cossack. Town Cossack Regiments of Western Siberia: Tobolsk, Siberian Tatar, and Tomsk, 1824-1825.

Senior NCO and Cossack. Town Cossack Regiments of Eastern Siberia: Yeniseisk, Irkutsk, Trans-Baikal, and Yakutsk, 1824-1825.

Cossack. Station Commands under the Troitsko-Savsk Border Chancellry, 1824-1825.

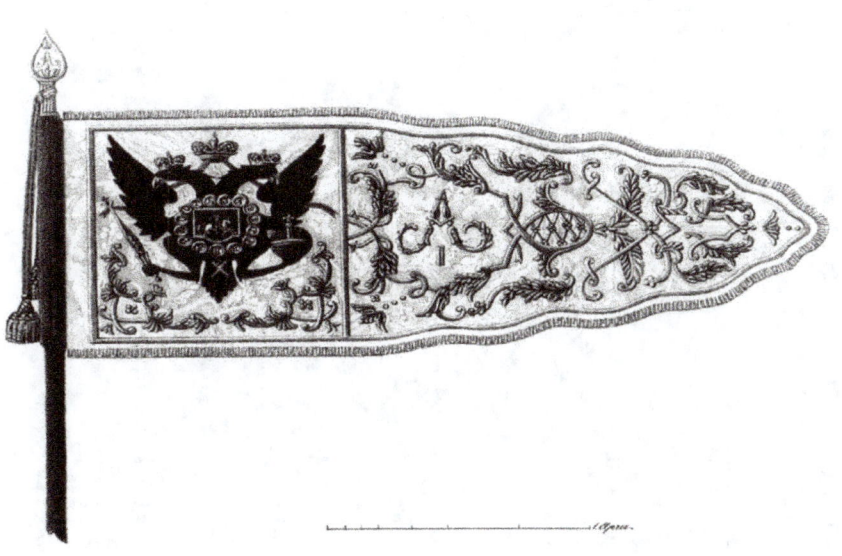

Flag granted to the Don Host in 1803. - Don Host Flag [Znachek], granted in 1803.

Don Host Flag, granted in 1803.

2493

Flag of the Don Host, granted in 1803.

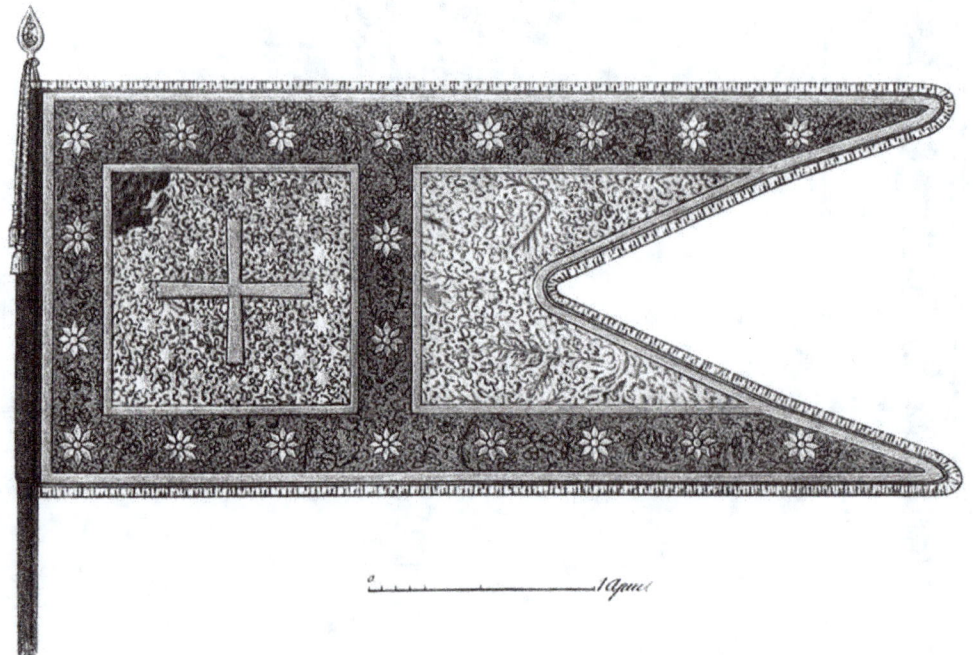

Don Host Standards [Bunchuki], granted in 1803.

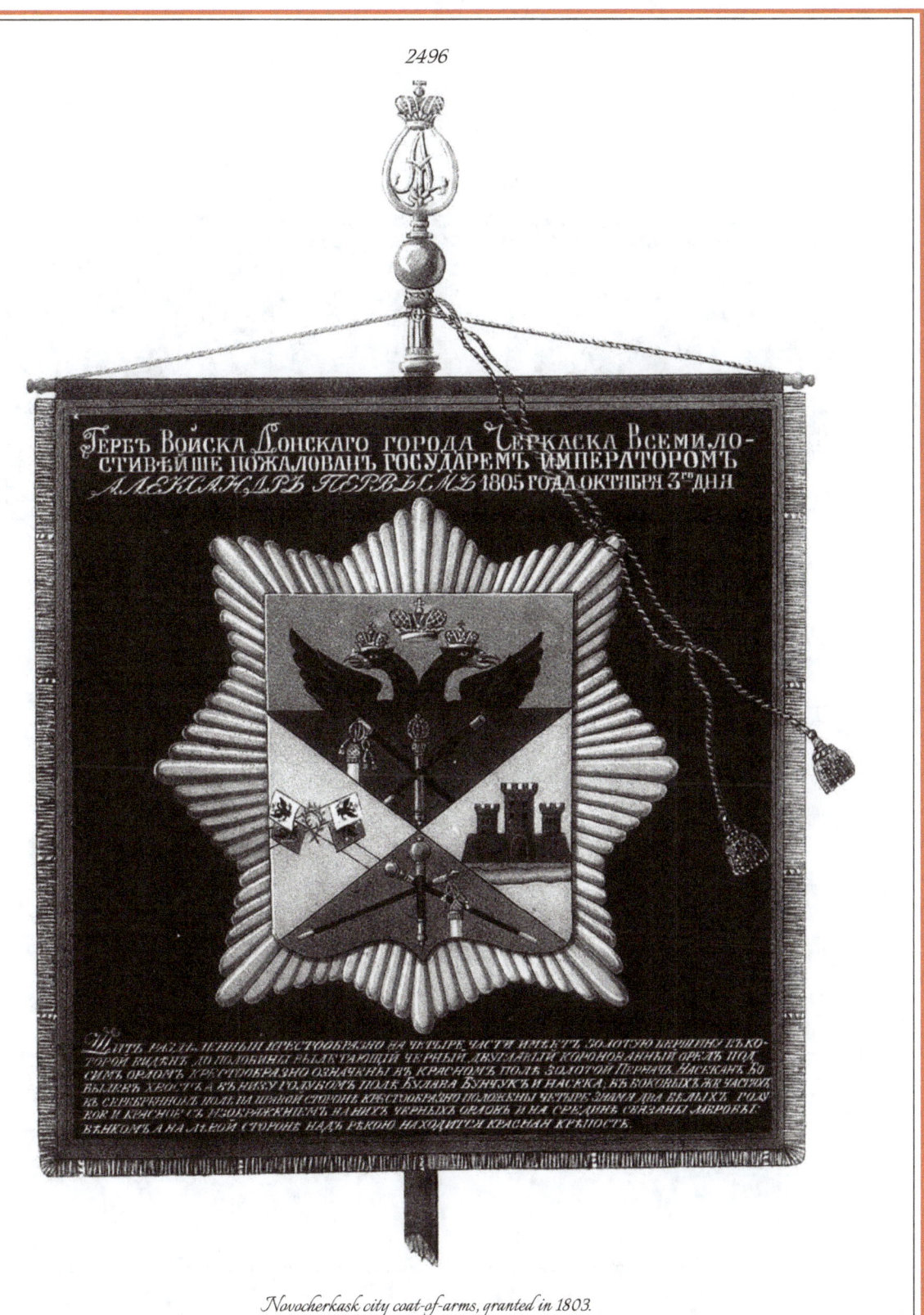

Novocherkask city coat-of-arms, granted in 1803.

Flag of Khanzhenkov's Don Cossack Regiment, granted in 1807. Note: An identical flag was granted at the same time to Sysoev's Don Regiment. - Don Host Flag, granted in 1811.

Flag of the Don Host Ataman's Regiment, granted in 1814.

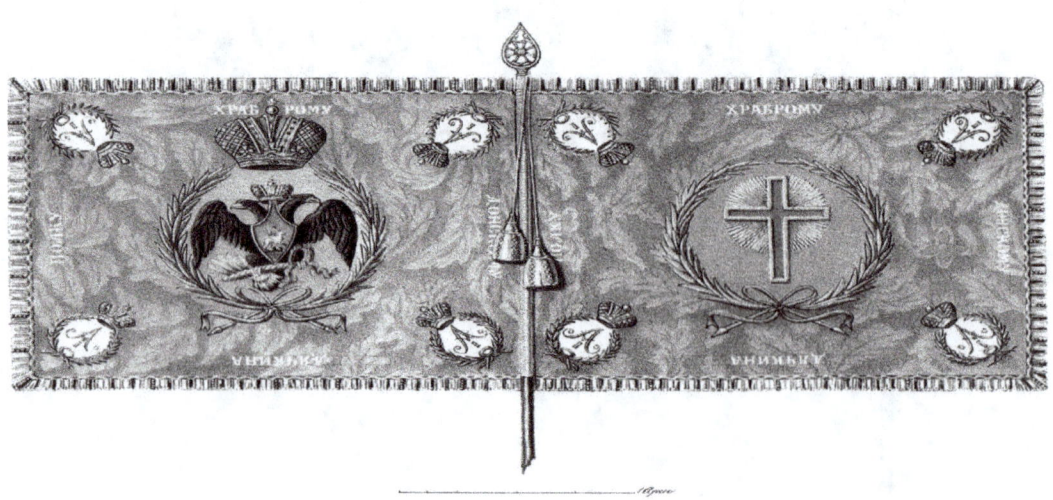

Standard [Bunchuk] of the Don Host Ataman Regiment, granted in 1814. - Flag of Dyachkin's Don Cossack Regiment, granted in 1816.

Don Host Flag, granted in 1817.

Flag of Zhirov's Don Cossack Regiment, granted in 1821. Note: The same Flags were granted at the same time to the regiments of Vlasov 3rd, Ilovaiskii 11th, and Grekov 18th.

12 вершковъ.

Flag of Mel'nikov 4th's Don Cossack Regiment, granted in 1821. Note: The same exact Flag was at the same time granted to Mel'nikov 5th's Regiment.

Flags of the Black Sea Cossack Host, granted in 1803.

Flag of the Astrakhan Cossack Host, granted din 1818.

Flag formerly with the 2nd Kalmuck Regiment during the campaigns of 1812, 1813, and 1814.

Flag of the 9th Bashkir Canton, granted in 1805.

Flags of the Bug Cossack Regiments, granted in 1804.

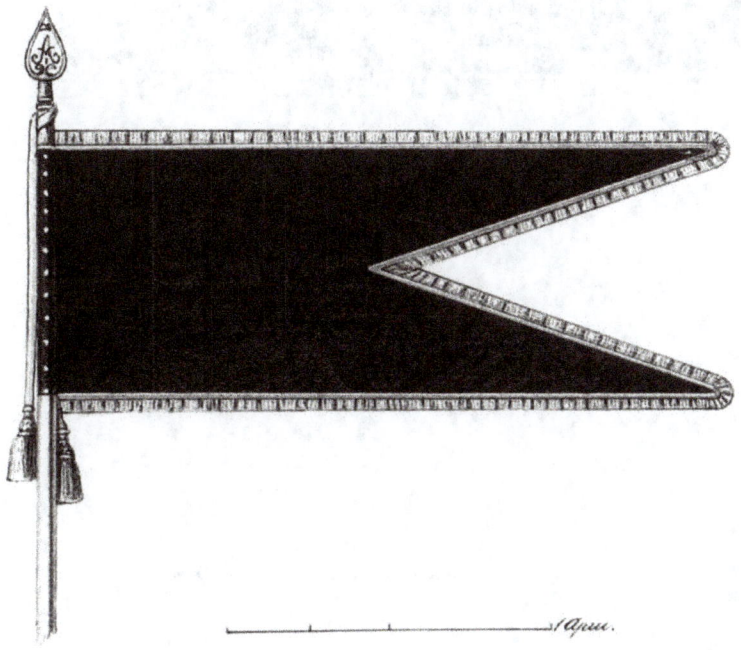

Flags of the Nogai Regiments, granted in 1802.

Flag of the Siberian Line Cossack Host, granted in 1809.

SOLDIERS, WEAPONS & UNIFORMS ALREADY PUBLISHED
(SOME TITLES)

UNIFORMS OF RUSSIAN ARMY IN THE ERA OF ANCIENT TZAR
FROM THE REIGN OF VASILI IV TO MICHAEL I, ALEXIS, FEODOR III DURING THE XVII th CENTURY
A.V.VISKOVATOV — LUCA STEFANO CRISTINI
SWU-600-004

UNIFORMS OF RUSSIAN ARMY OF PETER I THE GREAT
FROM THE REIGN OF PETER I TO CATHERINE I, PEER II, ANNA AND IVAN VI. 1682-1741
A.V.VISKOVATOV — LUCA STEFANO CRISTINI
SWU-700-006

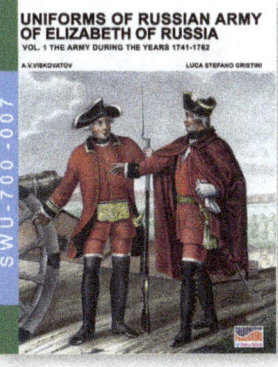

UNIFORMS OF RUSSIAN ARMY OF ELIZABETH OF RUSSIA
VOL. 1 THE ARMY DURING THE YEARS 1741-1762
A.V.VISKOVATOV — LUCA STEFANO CRISTINI
SWU-700-007

UNIFORMS OF RUSSIAN ARMY OF ELIZABETH OF RUSSIA
VOL. 2 THE ARMY DURING THE YEARS 1741-1762
A.V.VISKOVATOV — LUCA STEFANO CRISTINI
SWU-700-008

UNIFORMS OF RUSSIAN ARMY IN THE XVIII CENTURY VOL. 1
UNDER THE REIGN OF CATHERINE II EMPRESS OF RUSSIA BETWEEN 1762 AND 1796
A.V.VISKOVATOV – LUCA STEFANO CRISTINI
SWU-700-005

UNIFORMS OF RUSSIAN ARMY IN THE XVIII CENTURY VOL. 2
UNDER THE REIGN OF CATHERINE II EMPRESS OF RUSSIA BETWEEN 1762 AND 1796
A.V.VISKOVATOV – LUCA STEFANO CRISTINI
SWU-700-009

UNIFORMS OF RUSSIAN ARMY IN THE XVIII CENTURY VOL. 3
UNDER THE REIGN OF CATHERINE II EMPRESS OF RUSSIA BETWEEN 1762 AND 1796
A.V.VISKOVATOV – LUCA STEFANO CRISTINI
SWU-700-010

UNIFORMS OF RUSSIAN ARMY IN THE XVIII CENTURY VOL. 4
UNDER THE REIGN OF CATHERINE II EMPRESS OF RUSSIA BETWEEN 1762 AND 1796
A.V.VISKOVATOV – LUCA STEFANO CRISTINI
SWU-700-011

BRITISH ARMY UNIFORMS IN 1742
IN THE ART OF JOHN PINE
SWU-700-001

PRUSSIAN & AUSTRIAN ARMY UNIFORMS IN 1742-1770
LUCA STEFANO CRISTINI
SWU-700-002

THE FRENCH ARMY OF ANCIEN RÉGIME Volume 1
IN THE ART OF FELIX PHILIPPOTEAUX
LUCA STEFANO CRISTINI
SWU-700-003

THE FRENCH ARMY OF ANCIEN RÉGIME Volume 2
IN THE ART OF FELIX PHILIPPOTEAUX
LUCA STEFANO CRISTINI
SWU-700-004

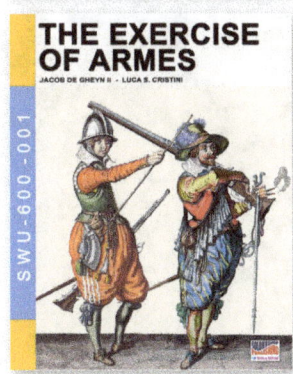

THE EXERCISE OF ARMES
JACOB DE GHEYN II — LUCA S. CRISTINI
SWU-600-001

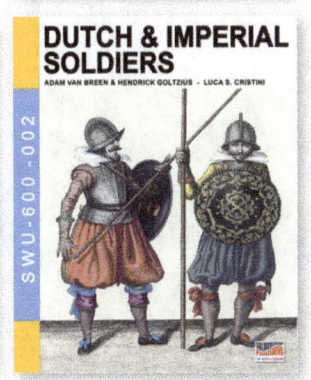

DUTCH & IMPERIAL SOLDIERS
ADAM VAN BREEN & HENDRICK GOLTZIUS — LUCA S. CRISTINI
SWU-600-002

HORSEMEN IN THE 16TH & 17TH C.
JACOB DE GHEYN II — A.DE BRUYN - LUCA S. CRISTINI
SWU-600-003

IMPERIAL SOLDIERS & UNIFORMS 1640-1860
IN THE ART OF FRANZ GERASCH
LUCA S CRISTINI — Plates by FRANZ GERASCH
SWU-GEN-001